Canyon Country
SLICKROCK
HIKING & BIKING

by

F.A. Barnes

An illustrated guide to
a completely different kind of
hiking and mountain biking
in the canyon country of
southeastern Utah

1990
Canyon Country Publications

This book is the TWENTY-FIRST in a series
of practical guides to travel and recreation
in the scenic Colorado Plateau region of the
Four Corners States

All maps, photographs and other graphics
in this book are by F. A. Barnes
unless otherwise credited

All rights reserved

Copyright 1990
Canyon Country Publications
P. O. Box 963
Moab, UT 84532

ISBN 0-9614586-4-X
Library of Congress Catalog Card Number 88-62755

CONTENTS

FOREWORD

This book describes a kind of hiking that is unique to canyon country, one that my wife and I discovered two decades ago and have enjoyed ever since. We have shared this special pleasure with friends, and now want to share it with the myriad canyon country visitors who might also learn to enjoy it, including both hikers and mountain bikers, and to some extent free-climbers, who will find plenty of challenges in conquering the region's slickrock domes, fins and slopes without the use of climbing aids.

As a youngster, I delighted in rock-hopping on the water-polished granite cobbles and boulders common along the streams and rivers of the Sierras, and climbing on the granite slickrock slopes exposed in the higher elevations of these mountains. There was something "neat," something that especially appealed to me, about running, walking and climbing on solid, uncluttered native rock.

As an adult, I rediscovered the joys of walking on slickrock, but of another kind -- the sandstones of southeastern Utah's canyon country. Most of the developed and marked hiking trails in this vast and spectacular region cross a little slickrock here and there, so most visitors have some idea about what it is like to walk on solid sandstone.

But there are also many place in this vast region where it is possible, and even necessary, to hike for many miles on almost solid sandstone, which is a special kind of hiking. It is special in several ways. While there are hazards unique to slickrock hiking, these are more than offset by the many unique pleasures that go with this distinct form of hiking.

For one thing, on slickrock the footing is firm. Also, there are many things to see that are not normally found while hiking more conventional trails and routes. A different kind of beauty is encountered and unusual things are found, such as novel erosional forms, geologic oddities, natural arches and bridges, springs in strange places, tiny, isolated plant communities, and both ephemeral and permanent pools of water, often teeming with rare and unique life forms.

Some of the areas where slickrock hiking is excellent are also good for a completely different kind of mountain biking. This was briefly mentioned in the book, *Canyon Country* **MOUNTAIN BIKING,** together with a couple of examples. This book lists many more slickrock areas and routes where this unique and more demanding kind of biking is practical.

Try slickrock hiking or biking, and discover another dimension to the exploration and enjoyment of Utah's canyon country.

Fran Barnes

INTRODUCTION

WHAT IS SLICKROCK HIKING & BIKING?

The origin of the word "slickrock" is rooted in pioneering history, although scholars are not all in agreement as to exactly why the term was used by those first to penetrate the vast wilderness of western America.

It is generally agreed that the term was applied to exposures of bare rock, but the mystery is why the prefix "slick" was added. Bare rock generally provides good traction to human feet, shod or otherwise.

The best clue is that bare rock does not provide good purchase for the hooves of shod horses, mules and oxen, or for steel-rimmed wagon wheels. Bare metal is, indeed, slick on bare rock. It doesn't give good traction, especially on harder forms of rock, such as granite, or on slopes.

Originally, the term "slickrock" was applied to the granite and similar rock commonly exposed in the Rocky and Sierra mountain ranges through which western pioneers traveled in order to reach their destinations farther west. In time, as the general Four Corners region became known, the term "slickrock" was also applied to the bare sandstone that dominated vast areas there.

Today, in the American West, "slickrock" is used to designate almost any sizable expanse of native rock that has been exposed by erosion. In southeastern Utah's canyon country there are countless such exposures of bare sandstone, varying in size from a few square yards to hundreds of square miles.

To the Mormon settlers and other explorers who first penetrated canyon country, its vast expanses of sandstone slickrock were formidable barriers or, at best, made for tortuous progress with their shod domestic livestock and their wagons with steel-rimmed wheels. Slickrock was a hazard to be avoided.

Today, however, canyon country sandstone slickrock is less of a barrier than an inviting challenge. The network of backcountry vehicle roads and trails left by mineral prospectors and cattlemen, many of which cross or travel on exposures of bare slickrock, have been used for decades by residents and visitors who travel the same eroding trails with recreational vehicles.

In a few places, new and very challenging routes into areas dominated by sandstone slickrock have been created solely for recreational purposes, such as the popular Moab Slickrock Bike Trail. This established network of marked routes in a slickrock maze was first established for use by motorcycles with off-pavement capability, but is now used largely by mountain-bikers. Other areas near Moab where there are large expanses of suitable sandstone, such as in the rimlands of Poison Spider Mesa, Gold Bar Rim and the Sand Flats, are also used for freestyle slickrock recreation, by a variety of off-road vehicles.

In contrast, few hikers who are not canyon country residents have discovered the unique pleasures associated with slickrock hiking, and few mountain bikers have accepted the unique challenge of freestyle slickrock biking. The purpose of this book is to introduce both hikers and bikers to this quite different aspect of canyon country recreation.

Lower Brinks Canyon

8

SOME VARIATIONS

Even in canyon country, with its vast and numerous exposures of bare sandstone, there are relatively few places where it is possible to hike or bike completely on solid rock, never setting foot or tire on anything else. It is almost always necessary now and then to cross patches of sand in washes, or where sand dunes have gathered. There are also occasional exposures within even the most barren expanses of sandstone where the hiker or rider must cross sandy native soils held in place by cryptogams and scrubby vegetation in order to reach the next dome or fin or ledge of slickrock.

The frequency of these interruptions in the bare rock depends on the kind of slickrock being hiked or biked. The non-rock patches encountered within all the massively thick wind-deposited sandstones are much the same, and these are closely similar to those found in the several fairly thick beach-sand deposits. There are generally fewer such non-rock interruptions in the ledgy slickrock deposited by freshwater rivers, streams, swamps and shallow lakes.

There are also apt to be changes in the kind of rock, and perhaps occurrences of loose sediments, at the interfaces between distinct rock strata. And, because of the way each kind of rock erodes, there are places within each otherwise hikable, bikable rock where there will be barriers, or impassable stretches.

For example, the more massive sandstones tend to fracture in near-vertical planes when undercut by erosion, leaving cliffs or slopes too steep to negotiate except with climbing gear. They also tend in places to erode from surface weathering into ledges, or into slopes too steep even for traction with rubber-soled hiking shoes or bicycle tires.

Unfortunately, the variations and discontinuities that occur within all slickrock create situations in which many areas that are fairly easily hiked, are effectively impassable even to the most skillfully ridden mountain bikes. Thus there are fewer slickrock biking areas than hiking areas. Further, because of variations in erosion between areas, no particular type of slickrock is hikable or bikable everywhere it is exposed.

For example, where not undercut in canyon walls, or jointed by ancient tectonic activity, the Slickrock member of the Entrada Formation erodes into gently rounded, terraced slopes that are largely negotiable by both hikers and bikers, although more of a challenge to bikers. When exposed in open areas, or where it has been jointed, the same rock erodes into domes and fins that are usually too steep-walled for either hiking or biking, such as in the Klondike Bluffs and Fiery Furnace areas in Arches National Park, except for limited hiking among the fins at their bases.

Thus, neither slickrock hiking nor biking is practical on all exposures of sandstone, leaving the selection of areas in which to pursue these two distinct types of recreation somewhat chancy -- unless you have a guidebook to help you get started.

For a list of slickrock areas and routes that are bikable, at least to some extent, see the special index in the back of this book.

Klondike Bluffs

SEASONS & WEATHER

Slickrock hiking and biking are generally delightful and practical year around, although during the summer months of June, July and August areas in the lower elevations may be too warm for some, and an occasional winter may have so much snow even in the lower elevations that hiking or biking of any sort becomes difficult or impossible.

Slickrock hiking and biking are also practical in all kinds of weather, depending more on personal taste than feasibility. Sandstone slickrock is not even slick to hikers when wet with rain, although there may be a little loss of traction.

Snow on slickrock is another matter, however. Slickrock surfaces with snow on them become very slippery, making slopes quite hazardous. With wet snow, even gentle slopes can be dangerous if they end in drop-offs. In very cold weather, snow becomes hard and crusty, making the snow itself slippery and dangerous, although hikers can negotiate gentle slopes of crusty snow by making deep foot imprints in the snow.

Since bikers have less direct control over traction variables than hikers, it is strongly recommended that bikers strictly avoid slickrock that has any snow, ice or even frost on it.

Thus, while heat and snow place practical limits on the ideal seasons and weather for slickrock hiking and biking, these limits are far less restrictive for these activities than for better known forms of canyon country recreation.

OTHER LIMITATIONS

There is one other major restriction to slickrock biking that does not apply to slickrock hiking. While there are many areas in this region's national and state parks and monuments where slickrock hiking is practical and permissible, regulations generally restrict the use of wheeled vehicles, including bicycles, to established and designated vehicle roads and trails.

Although such regulations may seem discriminatory, they are necessary in order to preserve park terrain in natural condition. Since it is rarely possible to travel exclusively on bare rock, as discussed earlier, wheeled vehicles such as bicycles are bound to leave long-lasting wheel tracks many places. Human footprints tend to "lie lightly on the land," and are gradually erased by wind, rain, winter freezing and plantlife, while wheel tracks in this region's predominantly sandy soils last for a long time, especially those that cross delicate cryptogamic soils, and tend to promote rapid erosion by channeling the runoff of rain and melting snow.

Mountain bikers are thus advised not even to consider slickrock biking within the areas noted in this book that are located within state or federal parks or monuments. This is indicated within the later sections devoted to individual areas and routes.

WHY ONLY IN CANYON COUNTRY?

Why are slickrock hiking and biking distinct forms of recreation within the Colorado Plateau region of the Four Corners States and nowhere else?

Because it is only here that a unique combination of geologic events have all come together. For a period of hundreds of megayears, thousands of feet of sand and sandy sediments were deposited by wind and water upon an ancient geologic structure called the "Colorado Plateau." Over still more megayears, these deposits were turned to stone and distorted by violent tectonic activities such as folding, faulting, jointing, uplifting, sinking and the formation of anticlines, synclines and entire mountain ranges.

The resulting distorted strata were then exposed and sculpted for still more megayears by water erosion and surface weathering, to produce the present totally unique land forms that now dominate the Colorado Plateau heartland of the Four Corners States -- the canyon country of southeastern Utah.

REGIONAL GEOLOGY

It is not merely coincidence that all of the more hikable, bikable geologic strata now exposed in canyon country were originally deposited during the long period of time when the ancient single continent called Pangea was still intact, when the present configuration of far-flung continents and islands did not exist, when there was no separate North American continent.

The basement rock of the original Colorado Plateau was there even then, however, and its western perimeter was part of the west coast of Pangea, sometimes exposed as broad, tidal plains or low-lying land, sometimes inundated by shallow seas, as the global climate changed and the sea-level slowly rose or fell.

Thus, during the 125 million year interval when most of the geologic strata that now provide the best slickrock hiking and biking were deposited, most of the surface of the Colorado Plateau was low in elevation and undisturbed by violent tectonic activity, with the highlands of the massive Uncompahgre range of the Ancestral Rocky Mountains to the east contributing great quantities of sediments to the lower regions of the Plateau. This permitted the deposition of thick, relatively uniform deposits, which in turn created the massive, relatively uniform exposures of sandstone that now make good slickrock hiking and biking.

During the greatest part of this period, the sediments were a mixture of tidal-plain and seashore deposits, some marine, some freshwater. Then, probably due to some long-lasting change in global climate, the coastal plains of the Colorado Plateau became largely arid, desert-like, for a period of some 40 million years, with the sea held at bay. This arid period ended with the brief encroachment of a tongue of an inland sea from the east.

During the 40 million-year arid period, the Colorado Plateau was dominated by thousands of square miles of desert dunes, much like the modern Sahara Desert or the more arid coastal deserts of Namibia, in southwest Africa. These ancient deserts, of course, bordered on the sea, so their dune-sands phased into extensive marine tidal deposits to the west, or occasionally in some other direction, and much of their mineral content was from evaporating marine tidal basins, with the minerals from solar evaporation carried inland by the strong prevailing winds, to mix with the mineral-sand in the desert dunes.

This high mineral content of the massive aeolian sandstones also ultimately contributed to their mechanical integrity, and thus affected the way they later eroded and weathered into shapes and configurations favorable to hiking and biking.

Thus, most of the basic factors that led to the present existence of hikable, bikable slickrock had their origins in geologic processes that began some 280 million years ago, processes that were unique to the Colorado Plateau. That is why slickrock hiking and biking -- at least on sandstone -- are recreations unique to canyon country. Unless you want to travel to certain remote regions of Africa or Australia.

HIKABLE, BIKABLE SLICKROCK STRATA

The following rock strata are the most often hikable when exposed on the surface by erosion. Some are also bikable in specific locations. The strata are listed from the youngest to the oldest, like a standard geologic stratigraphic column, with their ages ranging from about 280 to 155 million years ago (MYA). For various reasons, the ages shown for individual strata are only approximations, and vary from place to place. Some of the strata are adjacent to each other. Others are separated by strata that are not particularly hikable.

It should be noted that the following descriptions apply to the rock strata within the area covered by this book, as noted on the map on the inside-front cover. In other areas of the Colorado Plateau, strata with the same names may be quite different in composition and form. A few such differences are mentioned in the descriptions.

Hikers who wish to know more about this region's geology and spectacular erosional forms will find the books, *Canyon Country GEOLOGY* and *Canyon Country ARCHES & BRIDGES* informative and well-illustrated.

Bartlett North Rim

MOAB MEMBER - ENTRADA SANDSTONE   AGE: 156-150 MYA

This topmost member of the four-member Entrada Sandstone is largely white sand deposited along the shoreline of a tongue of an inland sea that invaded canyon country from the east, covering the remnants of the earlier sand dune region to just west of the present highway, U.S.191. It is largely white sandstone, since the iron oxide that gives canyon country sandstone its reddish color was washed out by shoreline wave action. The Moab member was deposited in a relatively level layer, but is tilted in many east-central Utah exposures because of subsequent geologic activity. Dinosaurs of various sizes occasionally left their foot tracks in the wet shoreline deposits of the Moab member.

The Moab member is the relatively thin layer of white sandstone that caps the salmon-hued Slickrock member in the general vicinity of the town of Moab, after which the member was named. It is especially outstanding in and to the east of Arches National Park and for several miles to the west of U.S.191, west of the park. It also appears along the rimlands of Wilson and South mesas, the two broad, elevated peninsulas that are visible between Moab Valley and the La Sal Mountains. This member is also exposed in western Colorado, in particular on the northern nose of the Uncompahgre Plateau to the south of Grand Junction and in Colorado National Monument.

As exposed, the Moab member is generally jointed by uplifting, but is relatively intact. Where badly jointed, it erodes faster along the joints to form a surface that resembles an expanse of immense biscuits.

Moab Member Entrada, Tusher-Bartlett Highlands

Where tilted by the formation of anticlines, as in Arches National Park, the joint lines sometimes erode into deep crevasses. When it is relatively level, this sandstone often forms water-holding pockets on its surface, some of them quite deep. Such pools often contain tiny ecosystems of their own during the late summer and early fall, with several species of cryptobiotic life such as tiny shrimp.

Most exposures of the Moab member are very hikable, and areas that are not too eroded are bikable as well.

SLICKROCK MEMBER - ENTRADA SS   AGE: 165-156 MYA

The Slickrock Member is dune sand that was deposited under extremely arid conditions. This is shown by the fact that the iron mineral in it is red. If the climate had been wetter, the red iron compound would have been converted to other iron compounds which are not red. Recent research has indicated that the oxygen content of the prehistoric atmosphere was probably much higher. Such an "oxidizing" atmosphere would also have tended to preserve the red iron compound in this and other ancient deposits. As in most desert regions, the dominant dunes were sometimes subject to the action of transient water, such as flooding from local storms, exceptional tidal invasions, or sediment-carrying runoff from higher areas. Thus, relatively thin layers of water-affected rock are often found within this desert-dune sandstone. In some locations these water-deposited layers are not red, but other colors such as gray, white, pale yellow or even blue. The Rainbow Rocks area to the west of Dubinky Well Road is an example of this.

The best-known exposures of the Slickrock member are in Arches National Park. The red sandstone fins in the Devils Garden, Fiery Furnace and Klondike Bluffs areas are this member, while the white tops on some fins are remnants of the Moab member. This member is also exposed in several other major areas, such as to the west of the park, on both sides of U.S. 191, and in the general vicinity of Wind Whistle Campground in the Canyon Rims Recreation Area to the south of Moab. It also forms the steeper cliffs below the rims of both Wilson and South mesas.

When exposed by erosion, the Slickrock member of the Entrada erodes in four distinct ways. As exposed in the heavily-jointed Klondike Bluffs and Fiery Furnace areas in Arches National Park, the Slickrock member has eroded into large, steep-walled fins. When this rock is part of a canyon wall, it erodes differently. There, if it is undercut, it scales away forming near-vertical cliffs. If it is not yet undercut, it erodes into complex, rounded terraces, with some of its harder water-affected layers locally undercut. In a few areas, the top of the Slickrock member is exposed. Where this occurs, surface weathering and water runoff sculpt the colorful rock into wonderlands of smoothly-rounded domes, basins, grottoes, canyons, towers, terraces, and myriad other esthetically pleasing shapes.

This member of Entrada Sandstone is generally suitable for both hiking and biking where it has eroded into gentle, terraced slopes along a canyon wall, and for hiking where a broad expanse of the top of this member has been exposed, leaving an open area of undulating "petrified dunes." Hiking is possible in some of its fins areas, such as in the Klondike Bluffs area and the Fiery Furnace, but is generally more demanding, sometimes making the search for a practical route quite challenging.

NAVAJO SANDSTONE   AGE: 175-168 MYA

Navajo Sandstone is also dune sand, but in canyon country it is generally white or nearly so, indicating that any iron content is not in the form of the reddish ferric oxide that lends color to so many other regional sandstone formations. The immense desert that eventually became Navajo Sandstone dominated the region for many millions of years, with its deposits exceeding 2,500 feet in places. To the west, the Navajo verges into shallow marine deposits, indicating that the region at the time was broad, low-lying coastal planes. Quite probably, the Navajo dune sand began as well-washed beach sand, with its original iron oxide thus removed. This sand was then carried inland by strong prevailing winds, to form thousands of square miles of coastal desert-dunes. As the sea level gradually rose over millions of years, the depth of the Navajo sands increased.

The broad intertidal region also contributed minerals to this desert, the "evaporite" ocean salts left in shallow tidal basins after the hot, near-equatorial sun had evaporated the sea-water. As these salts were carried inland by wind, they mixed with the dune-sand, giving the present Navajo Sandstone its fairly high mineral content. Some of these minerals were later partially dissolved from the sand dunes by rain and redeposited in ephemeral desert "playas," or shallow, temporary lakes. Remnants of these "petrified playas" now appear as relatively thin harder layers within the Navajo, where this rock has been exposed by surface erosion, or in cross-section in Navajo cliffs.

There were also occasional permanent water holes, "oases," in the Navajo desert, just as there are in modern sand-dune deserts such as those along the coast of northern and southwestern Africa, including the mighty Sahara. These verdant oases, with their pools and swamps of precious water, supported dense bands of vegetation, including tall trees and, no doubt, many species of animal and insect life. This left petrified logs and other fossils at various levels within the Navajo Sandstone.

Many such "petrified oases" have recently been discovered and reported. There are doubtless many more. Prehistoric reptiles of all sizes, including some that flew, also walked the Navajo desert, leaving their foot tracks in the muds of its oases and playas for discovery by human hikers megayears later. Several such sites have already been found in canyon country, and doubtless others still await discovery by observant hikers.

Navajo Sandstone erodes much like the Slickrock member of Entrada Sandstone. On exposed upper surfaces that are relatively level, it forms "petrified dunes" that are cut by canyons of varying depths. When it is jointed by tectonic action, such as in the vicinity of anticlines or other uplifts, it erodes into high, sheer-walled fins. In canyon walls, it collapses along near-vertical planes when undercut, but erodes into more gentle, rounded terraces and other shapes when not undercut. Like the Moab and Slickrock members of Entrada Sandstone, its upper surface readily forms potholes of various sizes that tend to capture and hold the scarce high-desert precipitation, at times reviving various forms of long-dormant "pothole life" from the sediments in such temporary pools.

There are many exposures of all four erosional forms of Navajo Sandstone in canyon country. The most obvious in the Moab vicinity are the soaring cliffs of the Colorado River gorge down-river from Moab Valley, the magnificent fins of Behind-the-Rocks, the lofty upper rimlands of Poison Spider Mesa, the "petrified dunes" area in Arches National Park, the immense expanse of rolling domes and giant fins in the Sand Flats and Mill Creek Triangle areas to the east of Moab Valley, and the hundreds of miles of rimlands in the nearby Canyon Rims Recreation Area.

Somewhat like the Slickrock Entrada, Navajo Sandstone is generally both hikable and bikable where its unjointed upper surface is not too badly eroded, and at least hikable in places where foot travel is possible between its fins. There are few places where the Navajo in canyon walls that have not been undercut provide significant hiking or biking opportunities. This tendency is largely reserved for the Entrada Slickrock, at least in the region covered by this book.

KAYENTA SANDSTONE   AGE: 180-175 MYA

Kayenta sandstone is sand and shale that was deposited by fresh water streams and shallow lakes and ponds during a period of wetter climate. The various layers within this sandstone are generally whitish or gray, but may also have a tinge of red in some locations. The sediments were carried into canyon country by water that fell on higher ground to the east of the region, primarily the massive Uncompahgre highlands. The wetter climate, and possibly the chemical actions of the decaying remnants of vegetation that grew in the area or were washed in from higher ground, changed any reddish ferric oxide in the sediments to iron minerals having other colors. Giant prehistoric reptiles left myriad foot tracks in the mudflats of the Kayenta, to be petrified then exposed by erosion millions of years later. One such set of ancient tracks is visible from Utah 279, downriver from Moab Valley, and there are others in the same general vicinity.

As exposed by erosion, Kayenta sandstone tends to form ledges and terraces in which the hard and fairly thick laminations are undercut where the softer layers have been washed away by rain runoff. This ledging is especially prominent in the myriad shallow gullies and washes that form when the upper surface of the Kayenta is exposed. Since Kayenta sandstone is water-deposited, and hence somewhat harder than the Navajo Sandstone above it, its surface, when exposed, resists erosion from flowing water more than the Navajo. This results in undercutting of the Navajo and its collapse into near-vertical walls.

This curious phenomenon is readily apparent wherever the Glen Canyon Group -- Navajo-Kayenta-Wingate -- is exposed, as it is in so many canyons in this region, especially in Glen Canyon, after which this group of sandstones was named. In such cliffs, the harder Kayenta layers protect the lower Wingate, which also sheers into vertical cliffs when undercut. On top of the Wingate cliffs, Kayenta sandstone forms terraces of varying widths, with steep-walled Navajo Sandstone set back from the cliff rim. It is this ledging that in places makes the Kayenta hikable and, in fact, such ledges often provide quite hikable and spectacular routes, midway between soaring cliffs, above and below.

The shallow gulches and washes that commonly form in the upper surfaces of Kayenta sandstone offer the best hiking, however, although few of these are bikable for any distance. Canyons cut into other kinds of sandstone often stop hikers with their sheer drops. While shallow canyons within the Kayenta also have sudden drops, this formation's ledgy nature almost always offers hikers a way around such obstacles. Typical hikable exposures of Kayenta sandstone in the Moab vicinity are in the higher country to the west of Moab, in the rimlands of the Bull Canyon-Sevenmile Canyon complex.

WINGATE SANDSTONE   AGE: 190-180 MYA

Wingate Sandstone is the principal cliff-forming geologic stratum in southeastern Utah. Most of the great convoluted cliffs that dominate so many canyon country skylines and define so many lofty, sheer-walled mesas and peninsulas formed from this rock.

Wingate Sandstone, like the Navajo and Entrada-Slickrock described earlier, was originally desert dune sand, although like the Entrada-Slickrock the arid desert dunes were sometimes affected by transient water. This left flat layers visible in present Wingate cliffs that are less permeable to seeping water. This also contributes to the formation of the immense seep-caves that are fairly common in such cliffs. As with the later Entrada-Slickrock, the climate during the Wingate deposition was hot and arid, and its vast area of dunes was low-lying and coastal. As with all of the region's "red-bed" deposits, most of the material that made up the Wingate came from the Uncompahgre highlands to the east, carried into the region by transient flooding, then worked into dunes by the strong coastal winds.

Wingate Sandstone erodes much like the Navajo and Entrada-Slickrock sandstones. When its upper surface is exposed, it takes the shape of "petrified dunes." When exposed in an undercut wall, it shears away into the near-vertical cliffs that are common to canyon country. When exposed in a canyon wall, but not undercut, it forms smoothly rounded terraces and shapes. When fractured by ancient tectonic activity, such as the formation of anticlines or uplifts, then exposed by erosion, it forms the same kind of sheer-walled fins that are common to the Navajo and Entrada-Slickrock sandstones.

Wingate Sandstone is different, however, in that its upper surface is exposed less often. The harder, water-deposited layers of the Kayenta tend to protect the upper surface of the Wingate from exposure, although there are quite a few such exposures in the Moab vicinity. Some examples are certain stretches of the Bull, Day and Little canyons to the west of Moab, in scattered areas of the Hatch Point rimlands in Canyon Rims Recreation Area, and adjacent to much of the northeastern rim of Cane Creek Canyon. There are other upper-surface exposures in canyon rimlands to the north of the Abajo Mountains. There would be more such exposures, in spite of the protective nature of the harder Kayenta deposits, if the Wingate were not based on relatively soft and erodable Chinle sediments. In most areas, these readily erode, undercutting and collapsing the Wingate faster than the Kayenta erodes away on top of the Wingate.

Exposures of Wingate Sandstone that are hikable are more common than is generally known, because most are in remote areas that are not easily accessible. Where they do exist, they provide excellent and challenging hiking.

WHITE RIM MEMBER - CUTLER FORMATION   AGE: 230-225 MYA

The White Rim Sandstone member of the Cutler Formation is the band of white sandstone that defines its namesake, the White Rim, the edge of the broad, winding terrace far below the soaring peninsula of Island-In-The-Sky in the northern part of Canyonlands National Park. White Rim Sandstone consists of off-shore sandbars and beach sands left behind by a tongue of the western ocean that penetrated only as far east as the present location of the Colorado River. Its thickness varies within the park. As exposed by erosion, White Rim Sandstone is relatively level and undistorted by tectonic activity, providing fairly easy hiking.

The lack of color in this sandstone indicates that any iron oxide that its original material might have had was removed by long exposure to shoreline wave action. As with the very similar Moab member of the Entrada Sandstone, when relatively level, White Rim Sandstone readily forms shallow pockets or "potholes," which catch and hold precipitation. There are also large exposures of White Rim Sandstone in the Maze District of Canyonlands National Park and adjacent areas of Glen Canyon National Recreation Area.

Virtually all of the White Rim sandstone that is exposed offers worthwhile hiking opportunities, but almost all of these exposures are within federal park or recreation areas, where wheeled vehicles are required to stay on established and designated vehicle trails. Therefore, biking on White Rim sandstone can be enjoyed only where vehicle trails cross or travel on expanses of this rock.

CEDAR MESA SANDSTONE MEMBER - CUTLER FORMATION
AGE RANGE: 256 TO 236 MYA

Cedar Mesa Sandstone, like most of the older geologic strata exposed by erosion in canyon country, was originally deposited along the shoreline of a western sea. Its white layers are wave-washed sands from beaches, shoreline dunes and off-shore sandbars. The red strata inter-layered with the white are sediments deposited in shallow shoreline lagoons and low coastal inlands by fresh-water flooding of the coastal areas. This horizontal red-and-white banding is typical of Cedar Mesa Sandstone, and represents a period of time when red fresh-water sediments from highlands to the east covered white shoreline sands, and were in turn covered by these white sands, as tides, winds and land erosional forces interacted for millions of years.

As Cedar Mesa Sandstone is exposed by erosion, it reacts much like the Navajo, Slickrock-Entrada and Wingate sandstones. Its upper surface forms a complex of rounded domes and other esthetically pleasing shapes. When tectonically jointed, it produces thin, steep-walled fins that sometimes erode further into graceful, slender spires. Along canyon walls, Cedar Mesa Sandstone erodes into the kind of sculpted terraces and slopes that make ideal slickrock hiking. When undercut by advanced erosion, however, it shears along near-vertical planes, producing the kind of spectacular cliffs typical of Wingate, Navajo and Slickrock-Entrada sandstones.

As with White Rim Sandstone, most of the Cedar Mesa Sandstone in the area covered by this book that has eroded into hikable form is within Canyonlands National Park, and is thus not accessible for mountain biking. Hikers, however, will find endless miles of hikable Cedar Mesa Sandstone walling the canyons in the Needles District of the park. The convoluted canyons of the Maze and its tributary canyons in the park's Maze District were also carved from this colorfully banded sandstone. The "needles" in the Needles District of the park are Cedar Mesa Sandstone, the upper ends of such canyons as Davis, Lavender and Salt Creek are walled with this beautiful rock, and many of the park's largest and most graceful natural arches, bridges and windows formed in it.

CUTLER FORMATION - UNDIVIDED   AGE: 250-236 MYA

Downriver from Jackson Hole and the potash plant at the end of Utah 279, the paved road that closely parallels the Colorado River below Moab Valley, the broad benchlands of red slickrock that extend back from the rim of the deepening river gorge are an undivided section of the Cutler Formation. In some areas, erosion has exposed the gray, fossiliferous marine limestone upper layer of the equivalent-aged Elephant Canyon Formation along the canyon rim, with the Cutler set back from the rim as low, eroded terraces and bluffs that offer good hiking and, in some areas, good biking, too.

This undivided Cutler sandstone is the typical dark red of iron-rich land deposits, with its material transported by runoff water from eastern highlands. Occasional intrusions of shoreline marine sediments are interlayered in the Cutler in this area, indicating that the land during that period of time was very little above sea level. The deep red color of the land sediments indicates that the climate then was very hot and arid.

This exposure of undivided Cutler extends downriver on the terraced benchlands of the Colorado River gorge for many miles, then for more miles it intertongues with the Cedar Mesa Sandstone that dominates farther south. The mixed layering begins southwest of a line that crosses the Colorado almost due east of Grandview Point, the southern-most tip of the Island-in-the-Sky. It ends along a similar line that crosses the river just upstream of The Loop, a large double-meander in the river. The broad band of red sandstone between these lines is just as hikable as the undivided Cutler upriver, and is also bikable over large areas.

The undivided Cutler, and its mixture with Cedar Mesa Sandstone, erodes on its upper surface into relatively flat expanses of red rock that is banded and mottled with other colors. As erosion progresses, it carves this rock into gullies, canyons, domes and terraces of every conceivable size and shape, producing some of the most colorful, wildly sculptured, esthetically pleasing rock in the region. This unique beauty alone makes the broad benchlands above the Colorado River gorge downriver from the end of Utah 279 worth exploring, although most access to this remote area requires a vehicle with off-highway capabilities. Mountain bikes can reach the area via the ORV trails that penetrate it, and can negotiate the eroded rock itself many places, but permit full exploration of this wonderland only when combined with hiking. Since almost all of this enormous exposure of ancient rock is outside of Canyonlands National Park, it is equally open to hiking and biking, with only the terrain itself imposing restraints.

ELEPHANT CANYON FORMATION   AGE: 280-256 MYA

The Elephant Canyon Formation is roughly equivalent in age to the undivided Cutler described above. It is largely marine deposits of limestones, sandstones and siltstones, with some thin beds of other highly mineralized rock of marine origin. Its various layers range in color from the pale yellows, ambers and browns of almost pure sand, to various shades of red and gray.

This formation is exposed on the surface in only a few areas in canyon country, largely within and adjacent to the Colorado River's inner gorge, from the potash plant at the end of Utah 279 to the vicinity of the Green-Colorado confluence. The formation is also exposed for several miles in Lower Indian Creek Canyon, where it has been uplifted by the Gibson Dome Anticline, and on the river side of Hurrah Pass, where the Cane Creek Anticline has arched various strata upward.

As exposed along the rim of the inner river gorge, the formation is hard limestone that contains a wide variety of shallow-marine fossils. The slickrock areas below Hurrah Pass, and in other Colorado tributary canyons are largely thick layers of red and pale-hued sandstone, with mottling in contrasting colors. Some layers are red with strange whitish pockets and striping that looks like marbleized cake.

The sandstone and siltstone layers of this ancient formation erode into distinct strata, depending on their resistance to various types of water erosion. In areas where the strata have been warped upward by anticlines, the formation takes the form of low-angled ridges of rock separated by narrow valleys of soils and sediments.

Where the Elephant Canyon Formation is exposed in canyon walls, it is generally too steep to provide practical slickrock hiking, but where it has been arched upward by anticlines, its tilted strata provide excellent opportunities for this kind of hiking, with a wide variety of sandstone shapes and colors.

OTHER FORMATIONS

There are, of course, other rock strata in canyon country that offer opportunities for slickrock hiking and biking, but the exposed areas are so numerous and limited in extent that it is not practical to cover them in this book. Once hikers and bikers have discovered the challenges and joys of traveling on and exploring the larger slickrock exposures, they will need no further encouragement toward extending their activities into the innumerable smaller slickrock areas. Sooner or later, almost all experienced canyon country hikers find themselves drawn like magnets to exposures of slickrock sandstone. They know that this unique kind of hiking provides the ultimate canyon country experience.

EQUIPMENT NEEDED

Normal hiking equipment is generally suitable for slickrock hiking, except that shoes or boots must provide good traction. Hard rubber soles, or soles that are smooth, will not grip the steep and often crumbly surfaces that are common on sandstone slickrock. Softer, waffled, rubber or composition soles are preferable, and in many locations make the difference between successfully ascending a slope, safely descending one, or not.

When hiking in slickrock that requires much use of the hands for scrambling up and down from rock ledges and through narrow places, some experienced slickrock hikers wear tough leather gloves to protect their hands from the rough stone, even in warm weather. Others also tend to avoid wearing shorts, in order to minimize skin abrasions from the close encounters with rough rock surfaces that are common to this type of hiking.

Certain optional hiking equipment will expand the scope of slickrock hiking, by allowing access to places and routes otherwise not practical for hiking. Climbing equipment such as lengths of climbing rope (25 to 50 meters), anchor bolts and tools for emplacing them, rappelling gear, and a geologist's hammer/pick, plus the training and experience needed to safely use such equipment, permit the ascent or descent of sandstone slopes or drops otherwise unsafe or impossible.

Mountain bikers who have had experience with Moab's Slickrock Bike Trail will already know the importance of wearing protective gear in case of falls. Such gear is even more important when biking on slickrock in primitive areas where no trails or routes are marked.

Biking on slickrock in remote natural areas is rarely along established and marked routes, and almost always involves the occasional lifting or lowering of the bike up or down ledges, or even carrying it for short distances over sandy or rough stretches. Equipment that facilitates such lifting and carrying should be standard for bikers who choose to pursue this demanding but highly rewarding variant on their sport. Bicycle tires that provide the best traction on rock are recommended, because on steep or lateral slopes good traction is absolutely essential to progress and safety.

ACCESS

As with much of canyon country, practical access to specific areas often requires the use of some kind of off-pavement vehicle. While a mountain bike is often all that is needed, some of the slickrock areas described later in this book are too remote for practical access entirely by bicycle. Thus, both hikers and bikers who plan to make a significant sampling of this novel and unique form of recreation must consider practical access before heading for a specific area.

While almost any of the many kinds of off-pavement vehicles, such as mountain bikes, trail-type motorcycles, all-terrain vehicles, dune buggies, high-clearance trucks and vans, and even some highway vehicles, can travel some canyon country backcountry dirt roads and off-road vehicle trails, all reach their limits sooner or later. Only four-wheel-drive vehicles engineered for backcountry use, and skillfully driven, can reach all of the areas described in this book. For that reason, the description format used includes an ACCESS section that notes the kinds of vehicles recommended for practical access to each described area.

Since it is not practical to duplicate in this book the basic access guidance already included in other publications in the *Canyon Country* series, another section of the description format notes the guidebook and matching map that contain detailed information about the backcountry roads and off-road vehicle trails within the various geographic areas in which the slickrock hiking described is located. The road and trail nomenclature used in this book is that standardized in the referenced guidebooks and maps.

While U.S.Geological Survey maps of the region show some of the backcountry roads and off-road vehicle trails there, they do not show nearly all that exist. They also do not name the roads and trails and many of the older U.S.G.S maps are seriously obsolete. None of them provide the mileages, pictures and detailed descriptions of each road and trail that are in the referenced guidebooks.

PERMITS AND RESERVATIONS

While permits are not required for access by vehicle or on foot into most of canyon country, special backcountry permits are required in the region's national parks under certain circumstances. Since regulations vary over a period of time, for current information, and permits when required, contact the nearest park office or ranger.

In some more popular park areas, such as along the White Rim of Canyonlands National Park, advance reservations are required for camping along the ORV trail during the main travel season. Reservations may also be necessary in developed park campgrounds.

Kirk Arch, Upper Salt Creek Canyon

HIGHLIGHTS AND HAZARDS

Slickrock hiking is not destination-oriented but rambling and exploratory. While it offers excellent opportunities for challenging and physically demanding recreation, the paramount benefit to slickrock hiking is esthetic. Hikers should be alert for natural beauty and for the myriad kinds of geologic and biologic novelties that are everywhere in the region. They should watch for human prehistoric and historic remnants, odd minerals, geologic and erosional phenomena and anomalies large and small, and for the various kinds of prehistoric and modern plantlife and wildlife that inhabit the region.

One of the pleasures of slickrock hiking that is not aimed at just getting from one point to another is the challenge of ascending to the top of every sandstone dome or fin, then safely getting back down. Every set of domes and fins also offers countless narrow and mysterious crevasses, canyons, slits and steep gorges, most of which can be explored. The number of three-dimensional strange shapes and forms that eroding slickrock masses can take is infinite, as is the potential for pleasure in exploring and appreciating these unique canyon country features.

Slickrock biking should also not be destination oriented, although in many areas it is so demanding of the rider's attention that if the true flavor of the terrain is to be experienced, bikers must stop and dismount frequently and walk around, to study and enjoy the same things a hiker would spot easily. Along a few routes, such as those that travel sloping canyon walls, a biker's goal may be to see how far along the wall he or she can safely travel, making the route "destination oriented" in one sense. But even in such cases, traveling the demanding route should still be subordinate to enjoying the setting and scenery. In areas, or along routes, where biking is more limited than hiking, bikers are advised to travel prepared to hike beyond where their wheels can practically go, and thus extend their enjoyment of the area. Although there is little danger of theft in the backcountry, bikers who wish to leave their bicycles behind while hiking can always buy peace-of-mind by chaining them to the sturdy juniper trees that are found everywhere.

35

The only significant hazards to hiking slickrock are places too steep for safe ascent or descent. Only experience can help hikers determine when a sandstone slope is too steep for safe traction, all the way up or down, and even then broad experience with the several varieties of rock, and how these weather on their surfaces, is necessary. A sandstone slope on one formation will provide far more traction than a slope of the same angle on another, and there are variations even within the same mass of rock. Since in many locations a failure in judgment could be injurious or fatal, it pays to be cautious when hiking slickrock.

Bikers must be even more alert for both sudden and gradual changes in slope while riding slickrock, since bicycles take longer to bring to a stop. Even steep upward or lateral slopes or rough stretches that would be harmless to a hiker can cause nasty spills that would be damaging to both bike and rider. Continual caution is necessary while biking unfamiliar slickrock routes or areas. Another precaution that bikers should take is to avoid the use of bike pedals from which the feet cannot be removed quickly. This has caused serious injuries to riders on the marked routes of Moab's Slickrock Bike Trail, and bikers on unmarked routes through wild terrain face even more such hazards.

Moab's Slickrock Bike Trail is a good basic training ground for freestyle slickrock biking. Bikers who are not already proficient on the varied terrain in that designated area, are not ready for the demands, uncertainties and sudden changes inherent in finding and biking over unmarked routes in "wild" slickrock.

Other than the steep and eroded nature of the rock itself, there are few hazards to slickrock hiking and biking that are not also present in other canyon country areas, and some of those hazards are even reduced in areas of solid rock. It should be noted, however, that some of the areas and routes described may not be enjoyable to individuals who are bothered by heights.

Even in slickrock areas there are frequent patches of windblown or wash sand, and such sand patches are frequently smoothed by wind or water flow, leaving them ideal surfaces for recording the comings and goings of the region's largely nocturnal animal life. Hikers who wish to get the most from their slickrock hiking experiences should be on the alert for such tracks, and will benefit from having studied a book on animal tracks, although even the best of these are lacking in high desert canyon country, since few cover the curious patterns of insect tracks.

Thus, all things considered, slickrock hiking and biking offer many advantages not found in more conventional approaches to these favorite recreational activities, and few of the drawbacks. Although the unique environment offered by slickrock is more physically demanding, it is also uniquely rewarding. If you have not tried exploring slickrock areas and routes, on bike or foot, you have not truly sampled canyon country at its best.

CONSERVATION

Canyon country geology is unique, and so are the various biological communities that inhabit some of its elevation ranges. Because most canyon country geologic strata are sandstone, its soils and other erosional products are either sand or very sandy.

As a result of this, the region's plant communities are delicate and easily damaged by erosion. Although the native trees, shrubs, grasses, cacti and other plants are exceptionally hardy and tenacious, whenever the slopes and pockets of sandy soils in which they grow erode away, their roots are exposed and they die, sometimes quickly, sometimes slowly. This phenomenon can be seen throughout the region. As vegetation dies or is diminished, the animal species that depend on it for nourishment also suffer.

Cryptogams are the basis for much of the plant-and-animal community within the more arid elevation ranges of canyon country. Cryptogams are a complex, interrelated community of microscopic plants that grow on the surface of sand and sandy soils, binding these surfaces tightly and thus preventing or drastically slowing natural erosion. The surface of cryptogamic soil appears dark colored, crusty and strangely textured. In higher elevations, the crust may have colorful lichens growing on its upper surface.

Erosion-resisting cryptogamic soils permit other plants to take root and thrive, and these plants in turn support the region's varied wildlife. Wherever cryptogamic crusts are damaged by human activities, the sandy soils are then exposed to drastically accelerated water erosion, and even some wind erosion, with the resultant losses of vegetation habitat and damage to the area's overall biological community.

Thus, damage to cryptogamic soil, the very basis of all other native life in the region, is not limited to the obvious and visible damage done, but is magnified with time. It is thus the kind of damage to the fragile nature of canyon country native life that those who care about the region's unique biological communities and natural beauty will wish to avoid.

Hikers and bikers who understand the importance of the cryptogamic soils they will encounter everywhere should make special efforts to leave them undisturbed, undamaged, even though this may involve taking a more circuitous route to stay on slickrock or in a wash with loose sand. A row of innocent-appearing foot tracks through an expanse of cryptogamic soil, or the ruts left by bicycle wheels, can lead to accelerated soil erosion and severe damage to the other plantlife that depends on the shallow soil, especially on slopes.

It may occur to some to ask why hikers and bikers should be concerned with conserving the fragile canyon country biological communities, when the land administration agencies responsible for its administration show almost complete disregard for this most basic conservation factor by "chaining" immense areas, and by allowing domestic livestock to graze every acre of land that they can reach. Since first introduced into the region, the grazing of public land has seriously damaged the region's native plant communities, and the hooves of cattle, sheep and horses do enormous damage to cryptogamic soils, thus promoting massive erosion. This damage can be seen everywhere.

For conservation-minded public land users, and especially those who use this land for recreational purposes, the answer to this ethical question is two-fold.

First -- many of the slickrock areas described in this book are relatively inaccessible to livestock, even though they may be within grazing allotments. Thus, slickrock hikers and bikers will encounter large areas of virgin, undamaged cryptogamic soil, and should take every precaution to leave such areas untouched. Even in level areas, such as in the large, shallow potholes that abound in slickrock areas, where the threat of erosion is minimal, the novel beauty of the color and texture should be preserved for it esthetic value, for the later enjoyment of others.

Second -- just because the administrators of public land do not respect its natural and esthetic values, and have traditionally bowed to the political pressures brought to bear by the livestock industry, does not mean that the public which actually owns the land must match this disregard. In this enlightened age, the conservation of all public land values must begin somewhere. Where better than with those who truly own the land?

SURVIVAL STRATEGY

It was the dead of winter in canyon country, and we were taking some friends on a winter-hike down a shallow but lovely canyon we had hiked before, in another season. The sky was gray with an unbroken, featureless overcast, a winter rarity in this land, except for the occasional storms that hurry through, on their way to some other, less fortunate region.

In canyon country, when we have a mildly cloudy day, we say -- *"Boy, somewhere is catching hell!"*

But, before I continue this small tale, a teasing question for those who feel they have a grip on the subject of high-desert ecosystems:

> *"What very common plant, that grows all over this arid region, and many others too, is largely dormant while other plantlife is green, growing and producing, yet is verdant and bursting with life while other plants are winter-dead?"*

I have asked this question of a great many canyon country visitors, while they were hiking with us through sandstone terrain thick with the plant, yet none have given me a straight reply. Can you, before reading on to find the answer -- and then still not understanding until I explain?

As we descended the terrace-walled canyon, walking now on water-sculpted slickrock, now on sandy sediments, we watched for signs of life. Nothing moved. All animal life was either sleeping or dormant. All the deciduous plants were bare, their dead and fallen leaves lying in brown carpets beneath their skeletal forms. Even the evergreen pinyons and junipers were a darker green, quietly musing over warmer days past, or yet to come. All life except us hairless apes was asleep, content to wait out the chill winter months in almost lifeless quiescence. All animals were still, all plants were seemingly lifeless -- all but one.

The layered Kayenta Sandstone that made up the walls of the shallow canyon formed undercut, rocky terraces everywhere, The canyon walls were a continuous series of stone shelves, some thick, some thin, depending on how long each rain had lasted, how much mud the runoff had transported into the lowlands of some primordial landscape, in some ancient time.

Most such sandstone shelves were bare, or sheltered tiny communities of cryptogamic soils, sparse shrubs and scant, dead grasses. All but one, that everyone spotted about the same time.

Under one deeply-undercut rock overhang we all saw a huge, glorious cascading mass of bright, chlorophyll-green, a verdant, living, thriving oasis of plantlife, supported by the scant snow-melt seeping to the surface of the canyon-wall.

Although my wife and I had hiked this way before during warmer weather, much warmer, we had not seen this spectacular array of verdure, largely, we knew, because it wasn't green then. It was dark-hued, gray, almost black. Dormant, when other plantlife was going through its annual warm-season life cycle.

As we continued on down the canyon, we started watching for more of this miracle-plant, this botanical eccentric. Once we knew to look, it was everywhere, green and thriving, even in places we hardly knew it existed because of its inconspicuous nature when sleeping through the high-desert's long arid season.

At last, we came to the end of our hike, a sheer, undercut pour-off into a deeper, lower section of the canyon. There, we gathered to-gether a big pile of dry twigs and small branches from a nearby dead pinyon tree, and built a warming fire on a sandstone bench in a slickrock alcove, where the next rain would wash across the terraced rock and carry the scant ashes on to nourish plantlife in the lower canyon.

After eating the lunches we had packed along, while warming our winter-chilled hands and feet beside the welcome fire, we climbed a narrow ledge that led out of the canyon to higher ground, for the return trip along the white sandstone that rimmed the picturesque canyon. Upper South Fork of Sevenmile Canyon was a nice place to hike, in any season.

Oh! -- What was that crazy plant that has its seasons reversed? In case you have not figured that out, it is *moss*. In arid canyon country, moss grows everywhere -- look for it whenever you are hiking, even through the most barren expanse of slickrock. But during the warmer, arid months, canyon country moss is largely dormant, hard and dry and black and lifeless-seeming -- and thus quite inconspicuous. Who sees black moss? Moss is green!

But following heavy rains, a relative rarity in this arid land, and during the winter, when the constant, seeping moisture that moss needs to thrive is common, it is conspicuously, gloriously visible, and as green as moss can be. Watch for moss, in any season, and marvel at another strange canyon country phenomenon -- a common plant with its seasons reversed for survival.

SAMPLE SLICKROCK AREAS AND ROUTES

INTRODUCTION

The following pages list a number of typical areas where slickrock hiking can be enjoyed. Some of these areas are also suitable for slickrock biking. There are many other similar locations, but those listed will serve to introduce the reader to this unique form of recreation.

The descriptive format provides useful information such as the kind of rock, bikability, maps, guidebooks, access, some on-the-ground guidance, and the area's special hazards and highlights.

It should be noted that many of the area names used are not "official," in that they do not appear on state or federal maps of the region. For purposes of this book, where official names did not already exist, the author assigned names based on nearby geographic landmarks.

The areas described are just that -- areas where freelance slickrock hiking and biking are possible and worthwhile for exploring by the more adventurous who pursue these two forms of recreation. There are also areas where the slickrock exposure is so elongated or otherwise formed that they provide clearly defined routes, rather than open areas with many routes possible. Such areas are defined as routes in the individual descriptions. There are also some open areas within which it is possible to define specific routes that offer introductions to the areas.

The areas and routes described are divided into six sections, which are the six major geographic areas in southeastern Utah's canyon country that are within practical recreational distance of Moab. Each of the six areas is covered by a guidebook and matching map, available as separate publications, which describe and show the perimeter highways, the interior roads, and the off-road vehicle trails that are usable for access.

Within each of the six geographic areas, the slickrock areas and routes are listed by rock type as an aid to the selection of places personally attractive to individual hikers or bikers.

ARCHES AREA

This geographic area is defined by Interstate 70 in the north, U.S.191 in the west, Utah 128 in the east, and the Colorado River in the south. The perimeter highways and the roads and off-road vehicle trails within the area are described in another *Canyon Country* guidebook and matching map. These are listed by title in each area description and on the inside-back cover of this book.

NAME - KLONDIKE BLUFFS

TYPE - area

ROCK - Entrada-Slickrock member and Entrada-Moab member

USE - hiking only

GUIDEBOOK & MAP - *Canyon Country* OFF-ROAD VEHICLE TRAILS - Arches & La Sals Areas and matching map.

VEHICLE - off-road vehicle

ACCESS

Drive the Eye-of-the-Whale ORV trail in Arches National Park to the parking area for the hike to Tower Arch, as described in the referenced book and map. Hike to the arch. As an alternate for highway vehicles, drive the park dirt road in Salt Valley to the parking area for hiking to Tower Arch. The hike from here, however, is so long that it leaves little time for exploring the Klondike Bluffs beyond the span.

Tower Arch

DESCRIPTION

From the arch, freelance explore the complex labyrinth of slick-rock fins in this area, where it is often challenging to find a feasible route.

To the north of the span, a canyon divides this area. It is possible to descend into this canyon, then climb onto the higher mesa of white Entrada-Moab member slickrock to the north. The panoramic view of the park and surrounding canyon country from this lofty mesa is magnificent, especially during the cooler months when the La Sal Mountains are snow-covered, and the mesa offers a multi-level maze of slickrock terraces and fins to explore. A slender peninsula of the mesa along its highest rim offers more adventurous hikers a spectacular view down the canyon that divides the maze of fins.

As an alternate approach to exploring this high mesa and adjacent maze of slickrock fins, drive to the end of the Klondike Bluffs ORV trail, as described in the same guide book and map, hike up onto and explore the mesa, then descend into the maze of fins. The route followed by the ORV trail toward its end travels along the tilted slopes of an Entrada-Moab member sandstone exposure that is also worth exploring upslope on foot.

View from beneath Tower Arch

45

NAME - K L O N D I K E R I D G E

TYPE - area

ROCK - Entrada-Slickrock member and Entrada-Moab member

USE - hiking only

GUIDEBOOK & MAP - *Canyon Country* OFF-ROAD VEHICLE TRAILS - **Arches & La Sals Areas** and matching map.

VEHICLE - off-road vehicle

ACCESS

Drive the Klondike Bluffs ORV trail, as described in the referenced book and map, for about 2-3/4 miles, to where it forks just before descending into Little Valley. Go right at this fork for about 1 mile to an ORV trail that goes northeast, to the left of the remains of an old movie set. Drive this trail for about 1-1/4 miles as it ascends a series of ridges, then descends steeply into a sandy wash adjacent to the white upper surface of Entrada-Moab member. Park and begin hiking here, or drive up the wash and park wherever convenient.

View of Klondike Bluffs from Klondike Ridge

46

DESCRIPTION

This complex 2-mile long ridge of slickrock is part of the tilted mass of Entrada sandstone that is exposed along the southwestern monocline of the Salt Valley anticline. Most of the Moab member slickrock, and all of the Slickrock member along this monocline, is within Arches National Park. The Klondike Bluffs and Eye-of-the-Whale Mesa are parts of the same monocline. The Klondike Ridge hiking area is adjacent to the Klondike Bluffs area, but is separated from it by an ORV trail and a major drainage line.

It is possible for hikers to explore both areas from a primitive camp established where the described access trail for this area reaches the wash, which is outside of the park. To reach a location more suitable for camping and exploring just the Klondike Ridge, drive up the wash for a few hundred yards, then climb out of it and continue for a short distance to where the ORV trail starts to leave the monocline and head down another drainage. This area also offers good camping and is outside of the park, as is the vehicle trail.

Exploring this slickrock area presents challenges, because of its sloping nature and the angled parallel jointing that have created a series of tilted ridges with narrow slot-like crevasses between them. The best way to explore the area is to hike the lower slopes, where it is fairly easy to travel, then hike up each ascending ridge that looks inviting. With some, it is possible to get to the next ridge from near their summits. With others it is necessary to backtrack. The challenge is trying to cut across the ridges at their higher ends, with minimal retreat downslope.

There are many highlights to watch for in this area. Turnip Tunnel, one of the few large natural sandstone tunnels in canyon country, is midway up between two of these giant, sloping fins. The upper ends of many of the more eroded fissures between the fins develop into complex and beautiful grottoes, caverns and slot canyons, some of which may contain narrow pools of water. There are several small natural spans in this maze of slickrock, some of them well-hidden, and another tunnel that is just large enough to crawl through.

Toward the higher, central stretch of the long ridge, the fins are too steep for hiking, but the canyons between them are echoing labyrinths well worth exploring. A few of these sizable canyons can be hiked and climbed to their summits, where there are still more lovely slickrock complexities, often set with tiny, isolated rock gardens lush with wildflowers in the spring, and views down into the colorful Entrada-Slickrock maze on the eastern slopes of the gigantic ridge.

In some of the larger alcoves in the central section of the ridge, rock ledges and potholes high in the cliffs are used by raptors and other large birds for nesting in early spring.

This isolated sandstone ridge is so immense, complex and beautiful that serious slickrock hikers could spend at least three full days just seeing its highlights, plus another day for exploring the nearby Klondike Bluffs.

Klondike Ridge, northern stretch

48

Turnip Tunnel

ENTRADA BERRIES

My wife, Terby, and I were hiking in a slickrock area accompanied by a professional geologist, who was also a good friend. At one point we came to an exposure of what have been called "Entrada berries," because these strange little spheres of sandstone are commonly found lying around on the upper surfaces of weathered Entrada slickrock. They also occur in Navajo Sandstone and, to some extent, in all massive desert-aeolian sandstones.

My wife and I have puzzled over these odd geologic phenomena for years, and I have sought explanatory references to them in geologic books and ideas from professional geologists. In every case, whether book or educated geologist, these and other similar oddities are authoritatively called "concretions" or given some other evasive technical name, but nothing is said beyond such empty labeling. No explanations as to how they formed. This is very frustrating to someone who wants to know the "why" of obvious and frequently encountered natural phenomena.

This time, fed up with the evasiveness of geologists and geologic books, I decided to take the bull by the horns and propose a possible explanation that I had devised, one that sounded far-out but that took into consideration all the details we had observed over our years of slickrock hiking.

As we walked through a large accumulation of little marble-sized sandstone balls, some lying loose, some still partly embedded in their sandstone matrix, I asked the geologist what these things were, and how they formed, adding " -- *and don't tell me what they are called. I already know that.*"

He had his mouth open to give the stock reply -- *"concretions"* -- when the second part of my question hit. He closed his mouth and looked baffled.

After several long seconds of total, almost embarrassing silence, I said *"Would you like to hear my idea?"* He quickly took this opportunity to escape from his dilemma, from the vacuum where knowledge should be, and looked at me expectantly.

"They're petrified hail-balls," I responded, waiting for the expected laugh, which quickly came. Then I said *"It may sound funny, but I am serious. Let me explain my hypothesis."* Which I then proceeded to do.

In desert-dune environments, violent thunder storms with attendant winds, rain and hail are fairly frequent even now, and doubtless were in the past. Such strong winds, shifting dunes and falling hail could combine to create the myriad sandstone "marbles" presently found in desert-aeolian slickrock areas.

50

In such a storm, the wind blows and the dunes shift rapidly by the mechanism of moving sand rising up the windward slope, then falling down the leading dune slopes. Then hail-stones start falling. Some fall on the leading, leeward slopes of the dunes. Some of these remain where they hit, on the slope of the dune, and are buried there, isolated. Others slide downward, collecting in bunches at the base of the dune and are buried in clusters. "Entrada berries" occur in such patterns.

Most of the tiny spheres of ice that have fallen on leeward dune slopes are buried unmelted -- a collection of hail-stones surrounded by fairly uniform sand that contains a small percentage of water-soluble minerals.

As the hail-stones melt, the surrounding sand collapses toward the center of each tiny melting ball of ice, creating a spherical volume of wetted sand. This wetting slightly dissolves some of the soluble minerals in the sand, and perhaps even a little of the sand's silicon dioxide itself. These dissolved minerals tend to bind the wetted sand together into a spherical volume that has a tendency to be slightly harder than its matrix when exposed megayears later to surface weathering.

Of course, by far the majority of such tiny subsurface spheres of hail-wetted sand are subsequently destroyed by the shifting dunes, or by other erosional or geologic activities. But a very few remain permanently buried, the geologically-slow chemistry of petrification takes place, and in some locations these myriad tiny "concretions," these "petrified hail-stones," are exposed to the wonderment of slickrock hikers, and the utter bafflement of geologists.

Since our geologist was a friend, he politely listened to my amateur hypothesis, but with visible skepticism. Still, I had started him thinking, and he was no longer laughing at my idea. Finally, I inter-rupted his bemusement by saying --

"This idea, crazy as it sounds at first, does fit all that we have observed about such phenomena over the years. I'm going to hang onto it until someone comes up with a better explanation, one that also encompasses all the observable facts. Do you have one? Or can you find a weakness in mine?" He didn't reply.

Do you, the reader of this book, have a better idea?

NAME - DALTON FINS

TYPE - area

ROCK - Entrada-Slickrock member and Entrada-Moab member

USE - hiking and biking

GUIDEBOOK & MAP - U.S.G.S 15-minute quadrant, Moab, Utah

VEHICLE - off-road vehicle

ACCESS

Drive north from Moab on U.S. 191 to where the Dalton Well ORV trail leaves the highway, about 11-1/2 miles north of the Colorado River bridge, as shown on the referenced map. Drive this trail in a northeasterly direction past the painted-desert hills visible from the highway, and into a shallow, rocky drainage. At a trail junction about 3 miles from the highway, continue in the drainage then steeply up an eroded ridge of dark red sediments that extends into an immense, sloping expanse of white Entrada-Moab member sandstone. Near the summit of this red peninsula, drive down onto the white sandstone, then follow any feasible route toward the mass of red Entrada-Slickrock fins visible to the north. Park anywhere near the fins.

DESCRIPTION

This large mass of Entrada-Slickrock fins and the broad expanse of sloping, white Entrada-Moab member near it, is another hikable stretch of the southwestern monocline of the Salt Valley anticline. It is an isolated continuation of the Klondike Bluffs and Klondike Ridge, and is about 3 miles northwest of Eye-of-the-Whale Mesa, the southernmost end of this immense monocline of Entrada slickrock.

Although the fins area is within Arches National Park and is also not bikable, most of the broad expanse of white Entrada-Moab slickrock to the southeast of the fins is outside of the park and offers several square miles of challenging slickrock biking.

NAME - E Y E - O F - T H E - W H A L E M E S A

TYPE - area

ROCK - Entrada-Slickrock member

USE - hiking only

GUIDEBOOK & MAP - *Canyon Country* OFF-ROAD VEHICLE TRAILS - **Arches & La Sals Areas** and matching map.

VEHICLE - off-road vehicle or high-clearance truck or van

ACCESS

Drive to the parking area for the hike to Eye-of-the-Whale Arch on the Eye-of-the-Whale ORV trail in Arches National park, as described in the referenced book and map. Hike to the arch.

Eye-of-the-Whale Arch

La Sal Mountains from Eye-of-the-Whale Mesa

DESCRIPTION

After viewing the arch, hike right, counterclockwise, around the slickrock mesa for a few dozen yards, to the first place where it is possible to ascend the mesa via a sloping sandstone ledge and then up steep slickrock slopes to the first broad benchland. From there, it is possible to explore this complex and enchanting square-mile labyrinth of slickrock in two sections. The smaller section is to the left from this access point, and enters an area of broad, sloping slickrock terraces above and behind Eye-of-the-Whale Arch. Several small but picturesque canyons carved from the same rock descend from here. All are worth exploring, but finding a suitable route down into some can be challenging.

The greater part of this area can be explored by going to the right from the described access point, then skirting around the head of the canyon that divides the immense slickrock mass. To reach the other side of this canyon it is necessary to ascend a seemingly dead-end terrace, climb up into a narrow grotto, then follow the only practical route up for a few yards before descending again. Beyond the end of this short route around the canyon head, it is possible to explore the balance of the maze-like Eye-of-the-Whale Mesa.

This is an exceptionally fine area for slickrock hiking, and offers at least a full day of enchanting experience, especially for hikers who appreciate the wide variety of esthetically pleasing shapes that eons of erosion and weathering can sculpt in the Slickrock member of Entrada sandstone.

Hikers with free-climbing experience, or who carry a length of climbing rope for short rappels, can descend into the lower stretch of the canyon that divides this immense stone mass, and leave via that canyon. This drainage reaches the Willow Spring ORV trail in about 1 mile. It is also possible to leave the mesa by way of a route that goes down a broad rock slope directly to the south of the arch after which this area was named. From either of these alternate exit routes, returning to the vehicle parking area involves hiking through the softer sediments around the base of the mesa, but also provides a closer look at its complexity.

Canyon within Eye-of-the-Whale Mesa

NAME - COURTHOUSE RIMS NORTH

TYPE - area

ROCK - Entrada-Slickrock member and Entrada-Moab member

USE - hiking and biking

GUIDEBOOK & MAP - any highway map of southeastern Utah

VEHICLE - off-road vehicle

ACCESS

Drive about 6-3/4 miles north from the Colorado River bridge on U.S. 191, then go east through the highway fence onto the old road that parallels the highway. Turn north on the old road and continue to Sevenmile Wash, then turn right down into the brushy bottom there. Follow this ORV trail for a few hundred feet, turn left and cross the sandy wash, then continue on the trail as it closely parallels the spectacular rim of lower Sevenmile Canyon. This ORV trail does not appear on any published map.

Lower Sevenmile Canyon

DESCRIPTION

The ORV trail used for access to this area continues along the rim of lower Sevenmile Canyon, which is rimmed with white Entrada-Moab slickrock. Good slickrock hiking begins at the breathtaking pour-off at the upper end of lower Sevenmile, goes for about 2 miles to its confluence with upper Courthouse Canyon, then continues up the rim-lands of that beautiful canyon for another mile or more.

These canyon rimlands, plus the immense triangle of Moab member Entrada slickrock that they define, offer delightful, varied and highly scenic hiking, with spectacular views down into both canyon systems. The walls of both canyons contain many dripping springs, and the ferns and other water-loving plants that thrive in such water-formed alcoves. From the area of their confluence, the immense cliff-wall alcove of Sleepy Hollow, with its large pool of spring water, is visible on the east side of Courthouse Canyon. In the winter, these cliff-wall seeps form gigantic masses of ice and long rows of immense, white icicles.

In the heart of the slickrock triangle formed by the two canyons, the eroded slickrock has formed hundreds of shallow, beautifully-shaped potholes, which hold rainwater or melting snow, some for long periods of time. During the late summer and autumn, many of these lovely pot-holes host the several forms of ephemeral pothole life that hatch from their bottom sediments.

The slickrock in this area can easily provide a full day of delightful hiking and exploring, and at its northern end also offers access to the uppermost end of Courthouse Canyon, where it first cuts down into the Moab and Slickrock members of Entrada Sandstone. The first mile or so of the upper canyon, while not strictly slickrock hiking, is well worth exploring. The stream in the canyon is heavily contaminated by cattle and its water should not be drunk by hikers.

While the eastern part of this slickrock area is within Arches National Park, most of the Sevenmile Canyon rimland is not and offers several square miles of challenging and very scenic slickrock biking.

La Sal Mountains from Courthouse Rims North

NAME - COURTHOUSE RIMS SOUTH

TYPE - area

ROCK - Entrada-Slickrock member and Entrada-Moab member

USE - hiking and biking

GUIDEBOOK & MAP - any highway map of southeastern Utah

VEHICLE - off-road vehicle or high-clearance highway vehicle

ACCESS

Drive about 6-3/4 miles north from the Colorado River bridge on U.S. 191 then turn east through the highway fence. Immediately turn south on the old highway and continue for about 1-1/4 miles to a vehicle trail that goes east. Drive this trail eastward for about 1/2 mile to where it joins another trail that skirts along the base of sediments that cap the immense expanse of Entrada slickrock that borders Courthouse Canyon and its several major tributaries. Park anywhere along this perimeter trail.

Courthouse Wash from Courthouse Rims South

DESCRIPTION

This hikable-bikable Entrada slickrock area is defined by lower Sevenmile Canyon in the north, sheer cliffs in the south, Courthouse Canyon in the northeast and a line of red-hued sediments in the southwest. It encompasses several square miles of complex sandstone that is cut by major tributaries of Courthouse, each of them eroded into a deep, three-dimensional maze of colorful sandstone.

The southeastern two-thirds of this area lies within Arches National Park, but the rest is open to biking. The park boundary is marked by small signs at intervals. The northwestern part of this area offers more bikable slickrock.

In much of this area the white Moab member of Entrada Sandstone dominates the surface, but has eroded away near the canyon rims to reveal the top of the more colorful Slickrock member. When the top of this member is exposed by erosion, but not badly jointed, it erodes into shapes reminiscent of Navajo Sandstone at the same stage of exposure. In this area, hiking is fairly easy, but the variety of rock shapes is still great, especially along the canyon rimlands, where water runoff has carved the rock into miniature grottoes and labyrinths.

Among the interesting things hikers and bikers should watch for are the shallow potholes that so readily form on the upper surface of exposed Entrada sandstone, and at least one natural arch that is visible in one of the several canyons that cut the area. The walls of these canyons also have numerous horizontal seep lines, where dripping water encourages the growth of water-loving vegetation, including ferns, mosses, columbine and other wildflowers. In the colder months, these long seep lines grow immense cascades of ice, and gigantic icicles, hanging in jagged rows like monstrous teeth.

There are spectacular views of the more familiar areas of Arches National Park from the canyon rimlands toward the southern end of this slickrock area. For an excellent one or two day hike through this area, drive northwestward on the perimeter vehicle trail that travels the interface of the slickrock and red sediments, to the rim of lower Sevenmile Canyon, then hike as closely as practical to the rims of Sevenmile, Courthouse, and its major tributary canyons, where the viewing is best. Return via another route and the perimeter trail, when it is reached.

NAME - COURTHOUSE RIMS EAST

TYPE - area

ROCK - Entrada-Slickrock member and Entrada-Moab member

USE - hiking only

GUIDEBOOK & MAP - *Canyon Country* **OFF-ROAD VEHICLE TRAILS - Arches & La Sals Areas** and matching map.

VEHICLE - off-road vehicle

ACCESS

Drive east on the Willow Spring ORV trail from U.S. 191, as described in the referenced book and map. Park anywhere convenient in the vicinity of Willow Spring, which is about 1/2 mile east of the western boundary of Arches National Park. As an alternate approach, drive west on the Willow Spring trail from inside the park.

DESCRIPTION

From the vicinity of Willow Spring, hike south into the immense exposure of Moab member Entrada that lies to the east of spectacular upper Courthouse Canyon. There are about five square miles of Moab member slickrock here to explore, with myriad complex drainage lines, erosional intricacies and colorful remnants of younger rock formations. Bordering Courthouse and the cliffline that defines the area to the east, more drastic erosion has exposed a maze of colorful, water-sculpted Entrada-Slickrock. Hikes along these rimlands provide outstanding views into the depths of Courthouse Canyon and of familiar park features to the north and east.

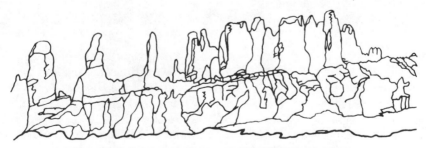

The Marching Men -- Klondike Bluffs

BEACH-BIKING

A west-coast friend once told me that " - *canyon country has everything but beaches,"* to which I responded, *"We have those too -- they're just a little older than yours."*

After he had puzzled over that conundrum for a few seconds, I explained that canyon country has several rock formations that were beach-sand when deposited millions of years ago. Such rock strata as Cedar Mesa Sandstone, White Rim Sandstone, the Moab member of Entrada Sandstone and several others less obvious in the region are largely composed of coastal beach sand, left behind when the western ocean advanced and retreated, or when arms of inland seas invaded the Colorado Plateau region.

Today, these primordial beaches, long since deeply buried and turned into sandstone, have been exposed by eons of erosion and shaped by surface weathering into forms that bear little resemblance to the original beaches beyond their bright-white beach-sand color. They might be called "petrified beaches."

A few such petrified beaches still bear traces of the prehistoric animals that walked such ancient shorelines -- "foot-tracks in the sands of time."

Theropod tracks in Moab Member Entrada

64

I introduced two mountain bikers to such a place several years ago, as we were headed for the colorful and picturesque Klondike Bluffs highlands to the west of Arches National Park. The ORV trail that approaches that elevated rimland travels along the western monocline of the Salt Valley Anticline, where a stretch of hikable, bikable slickrock extends for many miles.

As we first rode onto this enormous expanse of tilted white sandstone, the grade was steep, and the barely discernible route threaded through a series of huge boulders. Then, as we rounded the red-sand embankment of younger sediments at the top of the grade, I called our little group to a halt, beside a huge foot-track in the solid rock. There were still others nearby, and a long trackway made by smaller reptiles a mile or so farther on, in the same stretch of white sandstone.

Dinosaurs had trod this ancient beach! Lots of them! And their ponderous meanderings along that archaic shoreline had left rock-echos that we could perceive 148 million years later.

We stopped again at another place a little farther on, where several sets of trackways crossed and recrossed each other, and mused about how these great alien beasts had dealt with each other, how they had interrelated, one carnivorous species with another, because all the tracks we had seen were made by three-toed, bipedal meat-eaters -- a type generally called "theropods."

As we continued our trip to the Klondike Bluffs summit, walking the final stretch of highly eroded trail, we watched for other tracks along the same prehistoric beach. We didn't find any that day, but they were there. They were indeed!

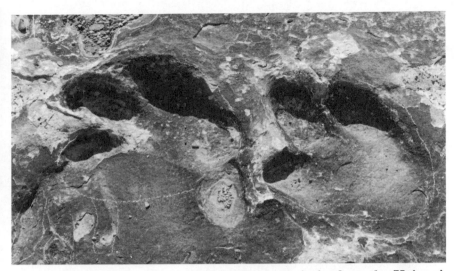

Several years later, a geologist-paleontologist from the University of Colorado found two other track sites several miles north, but on the same primordial beach. One had an amazing 2,300 large theropod tracks, many of them almost perfectly preserved in the white sandstone. The other had a couple of similar tracks, but also had several of the kind of massive, deeply-impressed tracks that were made by sauropods, those gigantic, lumbering quadrupeds with long necks and tails that are always so conspicuous among pictures of dinosaurs. These few tracks proved to be the first of their kind found in Utah --

-- and they were discovered in 1989 on an ancient canyon country shoreline!   " - *no beaches* - " indeed!

NAME - EAST ARCHES

TYPE - area

ROCK - Entrada-Slickrock member and Entrada-Moab member

USE - hiking and limited biking

GUIDEBOOK & MAP - *Canyon Country* OFF-ROAD VEHICLE TRAILS - Arches & La Sals Areas and matching map

VEHICLE - any vehicle for one access, off-road vehicle for access to the northern end of the elongated area

ACCESS

For access with any kind of vehicle, drive into Arches National Park on its main paved road to the parking area for hiking to Sand Dune Arch and Broken Arch. Hike to Broken Arch, then continue eastward onto the white slickrock. The area can also be entered by hiking generally eastward from the park campground.

Broken Arch

68

For access to the northern end of this long area, drive north from Moab on U.S. 191. Turn right onto Thompson Road, then east on the Yellowcat ORV trail, as described in the referenced book and map. After about 12 miles, where the trail is heading south, leave the Yellowcat trail and continue generally southward on a less obvious ORV trail, toward the red Entrada-Slickrock towers and fins of the Devils Garden section of Arches National Park and the broad expanse of white Entrada-Moab member in the near-distance. Park anywhere convenient and hike from there.

Other rarely-traveled ORV trails approach this long stretch of slickrock from the nearby Yellowcat mining area, but should not be traveled except on foot beyond the posted park boundary.

It is possible, with some difficulty, to climb up onto the southeastern end of this area from the parking area at historic Wolfe Ranch, the trailhead for the hike to Delicate Arch, in Arches National Park. A steep hiking trail that begins at the Fiery Furnace parking area also provides entry to the area.

DESCRIPTION

The Entrada-Moab member in this 12-mile long area is the exposed spine of the northeastern monocline of the Salt Valley anticline. It is cut by many lateral drainages, some shallow but picturesque, others deep and spectacular. Most of these drainage lines begin high on the monocline ridge, near the geologically older, but physically higher Entrada-Slickrock fins that are so prominent along the main paved road in Arches National Park.

While most of the hiking in this area is on white Entrada-Moab slickrock, some drainages cut into the older Slickrock member and thus afford colorful variety. The Fin Canyon drainage, for example, provides hikers a redrock maze to explore.

Most of this area is in the northeastern part of Arches National Park, but the northwestern end of the area is outside of the park and affords bikers a limited chance to explore the area. The referenced map can be used by bikers to determine what areas are outside the park, and hence open to biking, where the boundary is not clearly marked.

Clover Canyon Bridge

70

Hikers who enter this area from the paved road in Arches, via the hiking trail to Broken Arch, will be entering the 12-mile long area in its approximate center. From that entry, one of the first highlights is Clover Canyon Bridge, which is about 1/2 mile east of Broken Arch, at the head of one upper tributary of the Clover Canyon drainage. It is well worth the effort to get below this bridge, then climb up into the immense natural cave behind the span.

For a first sample of what this large, elongated slickrock area has to offer, hike on down the shallow Clover Canyon drainage, as it steps down repeatedly, enters a narrow canyon full of seep-fed trees, then plunges over an undercut cliff into lovely, verdant Clover Canyon. It is possible to explore this canyon, and its own large tributary, by descending into Salt Wash via the gas pipeline slope upstream of the canyon mouth.

The next canyon north of this one has a small historic building at its head in a grove of cottonwood trees, and almost every drainage that enters Salt Wash offers strange and beautiful examples of water erosion, with slickrock cascades, grottoes, deep potholes and spring-seeps in many places. Such dripping water is generally potable, if captured before it reaches the ground.

This long area in a relatively unknown part of Arches National Park is so diverse and varied that hikers can easily spend many days, even weeks, exploring its intricacies and beauty. For the more adventurous, backpacking may be the key to thorough exploration.

Hikers who wish to spend more than one day exploring this area can do so from a base in the park campground. Alternatively, both hikers and bikers can approach the area via the ORV trail from the north, then explore from a camp established anywhere convenient outside of the park. Backpackers could enter the area there, hike southeastward along its length for two or three days, then arrange for pick-up at Wolfe Ranch.

This is one of the longest single exposures of slickrock in the Moab area, and is largely within Arches National Park, yet is one of the least known. It is well worth exploring.

NAME - SALT WASH - LOST SPRING POINT

TYPE - area

ROCK - Entrada-Moab member

USE - hiking and biking

GUIDEBOOK & MAP - *Canyon Country* OFF-ROAD VEHICLE TRAILS - **Arches & La Sals Areas** and matching map

VEHICLE - off-road vehicle

ACCESS

Drive to the southern end of the Lost Spring Canyon ORV trail, as described in the referenced book and map.

DESCRIPTION

This relatively small area of Entrada-Moab member slickrock is outstanding in the views it affords down into beautiful lower Salt Wash and Lost Spring canyons, with their sloping, colorful, convoluted walls of banded Entrada-Slickrock sandstone.

The best way to hike this area is to park the vehicle as soon as it reaches the triangular white slickrock area formed by the confluence of the two canyons, then hike their rims.

The Salt Wash rim affords tantalizing views westward of the monocline in the eastern part of Arches National Park and the tributary canyons and springs at the lower ends of its major drainages. The Lost Spring Canyon rim provides panoramic views eastward into a colorful labyrinth of canyons carved from banded Entrada-Slickrock sandstone.

Adventurous hikers might find it challenging to see if they can find a way down from this elevated area, into either Salt Wash or Lost Spring Canyon, perhaps using climbing ropes and skills. Those who first documented large and beautiful Covert Arch spotted it from the ORV trail used to reach this area, just before the trail plunged down from the higher level in the red sediments. The arch is a gracefully arcing opening between two adjacent tributary canyons of Lost Spring, on the east side of the canyon.

There are two other smaller arches in the west rim of this canyon, just below the rim as the ORV trail closely parallels the canyon. It is possible to hike down to both of these curious spans. One was named Inchworm Arch, from its shape, while the other is called Silhouette Window.

74

Covert Arch

Inchworm Arch

75

CANYON RIMS AREA

This geographic area is defined by U.S. 191 in the east, Utah 211 and lower Indian Creek in the south, and the Colorado River in the west. The perimeter highways and the roads and off-road vehicle trails within the area are described in another *Canyon Country* guidebook and matching map. These are listed by title in each area description and on the inside-back cover of this book.

NAME - AMASA BACK

TYPE - area

ROCK - Navajo and Kayenta sandstones

USE - hiking only

GUIDEBOOK & MAP - *Canyon Country* OFF-ROAD VEHICLE TRAILS - **Canyon Rims & Needles Areas** and matching map.

VEHICLE - off-road vehicle or small boat

ACCESS

Drive to the end of the Amasa Back ORV trail, as described in the referenced book and map, then hike beyond that, or drive downriver on Utah 279, launch a boat at the Gold Bar Bend ramp, then boat upriver for about 1-1/2 miles to where the riverbank brush on the west side of the river ends at a Kayenta slickrock ledge, then explore on foot from there.

Amasa Back Kayenta Sandstone -- beyond river

DESCRIPTION

The vehicle approach is spectacular, and worthwhile in itself for those who enjoy a scenic, challenging trail, but may not always be passable because it fords lower Cane Creek. It is also hazardous where it skirts the high rim of Jackson Hole, a cliff-walled, abandoned meander of the Colorado River.

The boat approach requires a powered boat that can make headway upstream against the river current, in water that is quite shallow many places except during the spring high-water period. If the river level is low, it may be necessary to pull the boat up on a sandbar and walk to the ledge of rock that provides easy access to the high ground beyond the riverbank tamarisk.

From the end of the Amasa Back ORV trail, hikers can continue to explore along the lofty spine of Amasa Back, which is a narrow ridge of rock surrounded by a loop of the river. There are spectacular views in all directions. The uppermost slickrock domes are Navajo Sandstone, while the sloping, ledgy slickrock below the Navajo domes and fins on the east side is Kayenta Sandstone.

Several such exposures of Kayenta in the vicinity have three-toed dinosaur tracks in them, and several large arches have formed in the Navajo just across the river. Diligent searchers may find other tracks in the broad expanses of Kayenta Sandstone on Amasa Back, as well as more arches hidden in the Navajo.

Amasa Back Navajo Sandstone -- beyond river

NAME - BELOW HURRAH

TYPE - area

ROCK - Cutler undivided

USE - hiking and limited biking

GUIDEBOOK & MAP - *Canyon Country* OFF-ROAD VEHICLE TRAILS - **Canyon Rims & Needles Areas** and matching map.

VEHICLE - highway vehicle, but an off-road vehicle will eliminate a short stretch of eroded ORV trail

ACCESS

Drive Cane Creek Road into Cane Creek Canyon then continue beyond the creek ford on the Hurrah Pass trail. About 1/4 mile beyond the ford, hike or drive right on an inconspicuous ORV trail until it ends in another 1/4 mile on an expanse of slickrock near the base of a large and very colorful sandstone ridge.

DESCRIPTION

The limited biking here is along the series of gently-sloping slickrock terraces that stretch generally northward from the end of the vehicle trail. Hikers will find it worthwhile to explore around the base of the towering ridge to the east, and perhaps climb some of its lower slopes, before continuing generally northward from the ORV trail end along the same terraces.

Hikers will be able to continue their explorations beyond where biking is feasible by climbing across the numerous drainage lines that cut the slickrock terraces and by scrambling up or down the larger ones. Pools and trickles of water can be found in many drainages in the wetter seasons. In the winter months, these turn into white cascades of ice.

As hikers approach the higher benches of rock that mark the apex of this part of the Cane Creek Anticline, progress becomes increasingly difficult, but the numerous short canyons that cut into the rock beneath the highlands of Hurrah Pass all contain endless varieties of colorful and strangely eroded sandstone.

While this area is not extremely large in extent, it can easily afford an entire day of exploring in a unique and exceptionally colorful slickrock maze that is easy to reach.

NAME - B E Y O N D H U R R A H

TYPE - areas and routes

ROCK - Cutler undivided and Elephant Canyon Formation

USE - hiking and limited biking

GUIDEBOOK & MAP - *Canyon Country* OFF-ROAD VEHICLE
TRAILS - **Canyon Rims & Needles Areas** and matching map.

VEHICLE - off-road vehicle

ACCESS

Drive downriver from Moab on Cane Creek Road, then continue
on the Hurrah Pass and Chicken Corners ORV trails, as described in the
referenced guidebook and map. The various areas and routes described
are near these trails.

DESCRIPTION

The first and largest hiking area accessible from the noted ORV trails can be seen in the wildly colorful and strangely eroded lowlands below the switchbacks of Hurrah Pass, in sloping terraces set back from the Colorado River's inner gorge. This large area of Elephant Canyon Formation slickrock was exposed and shaped into its warped and tilted configuration by Cane Creek Anticline, a large upward bulge in the rock strata that is clearly visible below and upriver of Hurrah Pass. Anticline Overlook, the lofty viewpoint high above the summit of Hurrah Pass to the south, was named after this geologic feature.

The easiest access to this warped, multi-layered mass of sandstone is from the Hurrah Pass trail near the lower end of the relatively long, straight stretch of trail below the switchbacks. Although some expanses of this area may appear inviting to bikers, the tilted, terraced nature of the rock here makes access difficult for mountain bikes. It is thus recommended only for hikers.

About 2-1/2 miles from the summit of Hurrah Pass, and just beyond the junction of that trail and the trail to Jackson Hole that goes through a fenceline and down a small canyon, a spur of the Chicken Corners ORV trail enters a small slickrock canyon, just beyond where the main trail climbs steeply up a rocky slope. The slickrock terraces above this box-end canyon offer some limited but interesting slickrock hiking.

After the main trail reaches the rimlands of the Colorado River gorge, the relatively thin layer of gray limestone that rims the gorge is the upper element of the Elephant Canyon formation. It is highly fossiliferous. Along many stretches of this rim, collectors will find the fossil shells of muscles, clams, oysters and snails, as well as the cylindrical remnants of crinoids and countless other tiny fossilized sea creatures.

About 4-1/2 miles beyond the summit of Hurrah Pass, two short spur trails go to a large mass of red sandstone a few hundred feet to the left of the trail that offers some interesting slickrock hiking. The base of this mass of Cutler sandstone, on its east side, is riddled with a network of caves. Some of these provide access to the higher levels of the mass, which are interesting to explore. Some of the caves here are so deep and dark that flashlights help in their exploration.

During the warmer months, hikers should watch for rattlesnakes in the caves, where they seek respite from the heat. Snakes are rare here, but have been seen. When encountered, these tiny endangered reptiles should be left undisturbed. They are a part of the natural ecosystem.

To the east of the caves, there is a fairly large expanse of slickrock that offers biking on its several lower terraces, and hiking up into higher levels.

About 6-1/2 miles beyond the Hurrah Pass summit, there is an interesting natural span within a few feet of the trail called Rico Bridge, which formed in the gray limestone that rims a tributary canyon. For a good view of the bridge, hike down the nearby slope to the large alcove below the span.

Beginning about here, cliff-base hiking on Cutler slickrock is accessible from the trail. Park anywhere convenient and hike toward the base of the high cliffs to the east of the trail, then continue hiking along the slickrock that is exposed intermittently there, exploring up any canyons that are cut into the cliffs. In a few locations, it is possible to ascend to and explore higher levels of slickrock.

About 7 miles from the Hurrah Pass summit, the Lockhart Basin ORV trail spurs left from the Chicken Corners trail up a shallow drainage. A short distance up this wash, in a small slickrock area, remnants of an old rock corral angle across the wash. This wall is said to have been made by horse rustlers, to make a holding area for their stolen stock. The slickrock there occasionally has water in its shallow potholes, but now rarely captures enough water for any practical purposes.

For easy access to the large areas and terraces of hikable slickrock on both sides of the canyon up which the Lockhart Basin trail ascends, drive up that trail for a little more than 1/4 mile and park wherever convenient. Hiking the complex multiple levels of this area of rock offers a challenge, and excellent views of the lower terrain, of the distant river gorge and one of its nearby tributaries, and of Pyramid Butte and the spectacular cliffs of Dead Horse Point and the Island-in-the-Sky beyond the river.

Cliff-base slickrock beyond the Lockhart Basin trail junction is intermittent except at higher levels, which are generally difficult to reach.

The Caves

NAME - BEHIND THE ROCKS

TYPE - area

ROCK - Navajo Sandstone

USE - hiking and limited biking

GUIDEBOOK & MAP - *Canyon Country* OFF-ROAD VEHICLE TRAILS - **Canyon Rims & Needles Areas** and matching map

VEHICLE - off-road vehicle

ACCESS

Drive the Moab Rim ORV trail, as described in the referenced book and map. Park wherever the slickrock hiking looks inviting.

The ORV trail up Pritchett Canyon also offers access to slickrock hiking near the Moab Valley rim in this area, via a trail spur up a tributary canyon about 2-3/4 miles up Pritchett Canyon from the Colorado River gorge.

The Behind-the-Rocks ORV trail offers vehicle access to the area from the south. This approach route is much longer, but is far less difficult than the other two routes into this rugged area.

Much of the area may become BLM wilderness. If so, vehicle access may be restricted on one or more of these three approach routes.

Tukuhnikivista Arch

DESCRIPTION

Slickrock hiking in this area is quite challenging in that much of it is so highly jointed and eroded that its Navajo Sandstone slickrock has acquired the form of immense domes and fins that are too steep for hiking. This makes progress between or around such areas difficult, and necessitates more than the usual amount of hiking on the kinds of wind- and water-borne sediments that accumulate between such sandstone domes and fins.

Slickrock biking in this area is restricted to a few places. One is along the first mile or two of the Moab Rim ORV trail access route. The first mile of this trail is one of the most demanding short biking routes in the area, and is occasionally used for timed-run bike competitions.

Colorado River from Behind the Rocks rimland

Buttress Arch, Behind the Rocks

Another small area suitable for limited biking is along and adjacent to the Behind-the-Rocks ORV access trail, where it descends from the Cane Creek Canyon rimlands into the upper drainage of Hunter Canyon. The part of this area that parallels or approaches the Moab Valley rimlands is far too vertical and broken for biking.

One of the highlights for hikers to search for in this area is Pool Arch, a gigantic oval opening with a pool beneath it, both eroded from a large slickrock fin of Navajo Sandstone. The span is located near the southeastern quarter of the southwestern quarter of Section 14, Township 26 South, Range 21 East. This map coordinate can be plotted on the referenced map or on either the U.S.G.S. 15-minute or 7-1/2-minute topographic quadrangle map titled "Moab, Utah."

Hikers who wish to do any amount of exploring in this immense, vertical expanse of slickrock should plan on either backpacking for several days, or day-hiking from a vehicle-camp somewhere in or adjacent to the area. The area and its ORV access trails are on public land, where wilderness camping is permitted.

View of Behind the Rocks from Picture Frame Arch

NAME - HARTS DRAW RIMLANDS

TYPE - areas

ROCK - Navajo and Kayenta sandstones

USE - hiking only

GUIDEBOOK & MAPS - *Canyon Country* OFF-ROAD VEHICLE TRAILS - Canyon Rims & Needles Areas and matching map

VEHICLE - highway vehicle or off-road vehicle, depending on which area of this elongated, discontinuous exposure of slickrock is to be explored

ACCESS

Drive west from U.S. 191 on the Needles Overlook Road in the Canyon Rims Recreation Area, as described in the referenced book and map. Park anywhere along this road where slickrock can be seen to the south of the road, beginning at the Wind Whistle Campground. Hike toward the visible canyon-rim slickrock. The Needles Overlook Road is closest to the Harts Draw rimlands between the Anticline Overlook road junction and Needles Overlook. An off-road vehicle is helpful for getting to some slickrock exposures via the ORV trails that branch from the paved road and go toward the immense inner gorge of Harts Draw.

Macomb Canyon, Harts Draw Rimlands

90

DESCRIPTION

From anywhere along the stretch of Needles Overlook Road beyond Wind Whistle Campground, hike southward toward the rimlands of immense Harts Draw. Although the Navajo slickrock is not continuous along Harts Draw, it extends intermittently for several miles along the spectacular canyon rim. These rimlands are slashed by several sizable side-canyons worth exploring, and offer excellent hiking and outstanding views down into the 1,200-foot deep gorge. The westernmost stretch of rim provides outstanding views of the Needles district of Canyonlands National Park toward the west and south.

Hikers interested in descending into Harts Draw will find two routes described in detail in a Canyon Country Publications booklet titled **HIKING THE HISTORIC ROUTE of the 1859 MACOMB EXPEDITION.** Other hiking routes in the general vicinity are described in a book titled **CANYON RIMS RECREATION AREA.**

Historic petroglyph, Harts Draw Rimlands

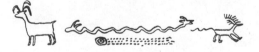

91

NAME - L O C K H A R T   R I M L A N D S

TYPE - areas and route

ROCK - Navajo Sandstone

USE - hiking route and biking areas

GUIDEBOOK & MAP - *Canyon Country* OFF-ROAD VEHICLE TRAILS - Canyon Rims & Needles Areas and matching map

VEHICLE - highway vehicle, off-road vehicle optional

ACCESS

Drive west from U.S. 191 on the Needles Overlook Road in the Canyon Rims Recreation Area, then north on the Anticline Overlook Road, as described in the referenced book and map. There are two access points to this long canyon-rim stretch of slickrock, with extensive slickrock biking areas at each end of the hiking route.

For access to the southern end of the route, drive north on Anticline Road, then park at the photographic pull-out 2-1/2 miles from the road junction. Walk a few yards farther north on the road, then hike west down the slope onto the red-banded dome of slickrock there.

Hikers should walk around the dome on the broadest terrace of red sandstone, then descend from its end to the rounded, sloped level of the sandstone. Bikers should walk or carry their bikes down to the left of the banded dome, onto the enormous stretch of bikable slickrock that is around the base of the banded dome and on to the south along the cliff-base.

For access to the northern end of this slickrock route, drive about 9 miles north of the Needles-Anticline junction then west on the Hatch Point ORV trail toward the Canyonlands Overlook. Highway vehicles can travel this ORV trail for a short distance but should then be parked. Off-road vehicles can continue to where the hiking and biking begin, where the ORV trail crosses an expanse of low, white Navajo Sandstone domes, about 1 mile from the Anticline Overlook Road.

At this point, both hikers and bikers should go south for a few hundred yards to the rimlands, then descend to the lower slickrock slopes that offer an extensive biking area and a route on south below the rim for hikers.

DESCRIPTION

Most of this miles-long, convoluted stretch of terraced and domed slickrock is at an intermediate level between the high rim and a broad, lower bench of Hatch Point, with outstanding views of Canyon-lands National Park and vicinity beyond the bench to the west.

93

It is possible to hike continuously from either of the access points described via this intermediate level of slickrock, except that it is not practical to circumnavigate a large prominence about midway, around which the slickrock walls are too steep for practical hiking. There, the best route is to ascend and cross the neck of the prominence, then descend to the hikable slickrock levels on the other side.

Along the way, there are several challenges to easy progress where larger drainages have cut into the curving terraces of slickrock. At such points, it is generally necessary to ascend or descend to where it is feasible to cross. Some such drainages are worth exploring in themselves.

More experienced bikers may find it challenging to travel this elongated, convoluted terrace of Navajo Sandstone slickrock as far as practical, beginning at either end.

NAME - TROUGH SPRINGS RIMLANDS

TYPE - areas and route

ROCK - Navajo Sandstone

USE - hiking route and biking areas

GUIDEBOOK & MAP - *Canyon Country* OFF-ROAD VEHICLE TRAILS - Canyon Rims & Needles Areas and matching map

VEHICLE - highway vehicle or off-road vehicle for one biking area

ACCESS

Drive west from U.S. 191 on the Needles Overlook Road in the Canyon Rims Recreation Area, then north on the Anticline Overlook Road, as described in the referenced book and map. After about 9 miles from the junction of these two roads, drive east into the Hatch Point Campground. Park and hike north down onto the slickrock slope below the campground, then east along its contours toward the distant Trough Springs Canyon rimlands.

For access to the closest of the two biking areas, walk a few yards down the slickrock drainage near the campground registration stand onto the broad expanse of sloping slickrock just below the campground.

For access to an even larger area suitable for mountain biking, drive down into the lowlands below the campground on the ORV trail that spurs from the campground entrance road just before that road goes through the fenceline protecting the campground from grazing cattle. Continue northward on this ORV trail for about 1-1/2 miles from the junction, then take a spur trail eastward for about 1 more mile, toward the base of the sloping sandstone masses to the southeast of the trail. Walk or carry bicycles the remaining short distance across the meadow then up into the slickrock in the vicinity of a major drainage line that divides the best biking area into two parts.

DESCRIPTION

This is another slickrock route within the Canyon Rims Recreation Area. From anywhere in the Hatch Point Campground, hike down the slope to the north onto the slope of Navajo Sandstone at the base of the bluff on which the campground is located, then hike generally eastward along the slickrock contours. Mountain bikers will find a rolling, smoothly contoured slickrock gymnasium area about 1/4 mile long within a few yards of the campground. A second such even larger area is farther along the hikable stretch of slickrock, but is better accessed from an ORV trail that approaches it closely. Bikers should not attempt to ride between the two bikable slickrock areas. There are stretches that are difficult for bikes and too many areas of sand and cryptogamic soil that would be damaged by wheel tracks.

The slickrock on the first mile or so of this route follows a rather convoluted route, and is broken by drainage lines with patches of soils, but then becomes almost solid rock. The broad meadowlands below the broad band of terraced, sloping sandstone is set with smaller domes of Navajo sandstone, and one of the ubiquitous bone-dry "stock-ponds" common to the region.

After a mile or so, one of the upper drainage canyons of immense Trough Springs Canyon, which is a tributary of Cane Creek Canyon, becomes apparent, slicing across the rolling meadows. After about 2 miles of hiking, an area of beautifully eroded and unusually colored sandstone is reached. Here, the whitish Navajo sandstone is intricately tinted with countless salmon-hued bands and eroded into great masses and gently rolling slopes and smooth drainages, providing a complex, three-dimensional playground for mountain bikers. A few hundred

yards farther on, the hiking-biking route crosses a steep drainage, then enters more of the same kind of rock, with still more outstanding biking opportunities. Easy access to this split area for bikers is via an ORV trail that crosses the meadows below, and is described in ACCESS.

Not far beyond this large bikable area, the sandstone slope rounds a promontory and travels the rimlands of another upper tributary of Trough Springs Canyon, offering spectacular views down into that canyon as well as a segment of immense Cane Creek Canyon. From this part of the route, there are spectacular views of the canyon system below, the continuing hikable slickrock slopes beyond the nearest canyon, the immense slickrock wilderness beyond Cane Creek Canyon, and the distant La Sal Mountains.

The route to this point or perhaps a bit farther makes a comfortable one-day hike, with plenty of time for exploring the colorful caves and other interesting features along the way, including beautiful Columbine Cave at the base of the slickrock in this vicinity. A two-day backpack hike will permit a longer and still more rewarding exploration of this route, around the noted Trough Springs tributary, then along the high slickrock rimlands above still another spur of Trough Springs Canyon, with still more enchanting views of the massive canyon system below and still other strange erosional features.

As an alternate to backpacking along this hiking route, for a second day of day-hiking, drive from the campground on the ORV trail to the tip of the mesa above Columbine Cave, then hike down and continue where the previous day's hike ended. This ORV trail can be traveled by carefully driven, high-clearance highway vehicles.

Columbine Cave

97

Views from Trough Springs Rimlands

LEARNING CURVE

We have a young friend who is a mountain-biking enthusiast. We took her camping with us once while we were exploring the backcountry ORV trails in the Canyon Rims Recreation Area, gathering information for a book about that spectacular but little-known region of skyscraping mesas, deep gorges and brilliantly colorful vistas. We wanted to show her several nice slickrock biking "gymnasiums" we had found on our last trip to the area, one of them adjacent to the campground we usually used.

Since we wanted to get some pictures of her for this book, and the late afternoon sun provided more dramatic lighting, we spent the day hiking a nearby slickrock mass and sharing some other local highlights with our friend. She was also an excellent hiking companion, and had accompanied us before into slickrock areas where bikes are impractical.

Late that day, after we had eaten, we showed our friend where she might like to try her first attempt at biking an unmarked slickrock gymnasium -- a large expanse of sloping, rounded Navajo Sandstone immediately below the campground. After she had donned her helmet and other safety gear, we all headed down the slope, with our friend walking her bike down the short, rocky gully that gave access to the slickrock.

There, as I got my camera ready and searched for an interesting and varied configuration of sandstone with a photogenic background, she cautiously peddled around on the gentler slopes, getting the feel of terrain that was not even approximately level for more that a few feet here and there.

Finally, positioned in a good place for a picture sequence, I waved her down toward the chosen area, a broad sandstone fin with nice color-banding, a route down and across to another sloping fin, and then back up again. After a lot of arm-waving she seemed to understand what I wanted and set out downslope, very cautiously, then back up the wrong way. I got one shot, but missed the best angle because she had apparently misunderstood my semaphored directions.

We tried again, and again -- but each time she seemed to chose a different route, or try the correct one, run into difficulty and have to stop. My wife walked over to see if she could better translate my arm-waving, and came back with news. Our athletic young friend was having a problem traversing the fairly steep slope before climbing back up the second fin. She was going slowly for my pictures, and not gaining enough momentum to cross the steep lateral slope to the next fin without pedaling -- and her uphill pedal was hitting the rock and tripping her.

My fault! I felt bad about contributing still more to the usual problems associated with learning how to handle a bike on roller-coaster sandstone terrain, so then gave directions that should be easier to follow:

"Just go and have fun, over in that area somewhere. I'll chase around and watch for good pictures."

She did and I did. And as the sun approached the horizon and the lighting grew still more dramatic, I got many excellent shots --- and our friend was able to learn and practice the special techniques needed for this kind of biking. Evidently she enjoyed the experience, because she was still at it when the sun finally set and dusk set in.

When she finally rode up to us in the gathering darkness, our biker friend's happy grin told us that she was, indeed, enthusiastic about her first sampling of mountain biking in one of the slickrock gymnasiums that are so plentiful, challenging and unique to canyon country. She liked it. She liked it a lot!

NAME - FLAT-IRON RIDGE

TYPE - area

ROCK - Navajo Sandstone

USE - hiking only

GUIDEBOOK & MAP - *Canyon Country* OFF-ROAD VEHICLE TRAILS - **Canyon Rims & Needles Areas** and matching map

VEHICLE - highway vehicle

Triplet Spires, south end of Flat Iron Ridge
The far spire is double

102

ACCESS

Drive west from U.S. 191 on the Needles Overlook Road in Canyon Rims Recreation Area, then north on the Anticline Overlook Road, as described in the referenced book and map. About 14 miles from the junction of these two roads, watch for a roadside pullout near a low sandstone butte to the west of the road that has two natural spans in its rim, one of them called The Wine Glass. From this vicinity, two dirt roads go east toward an immense, elongated mass of hikable slickrock.

The road that approaches the northern end of the slickrock can be traveled by carefully driven highway vehicles almost to the base of the rock, and off-road vehicles can continue to its northern end, but access up onto the slickrock is difficult from this end.

The road that goes to the southern end of the hikable slickrock first heads toward an industrial installation as a wide road, but within a few yards angles left as a narrow graded dirt road to continue toward the slickrock mass. This road ends at a small reservoir at the base of the rock.

Access from this road up onto the great mass of slickrock is not easy, but is possible three places at or near the south end. One is up a steep slope at the south end, from near the road. Another is just north of the reservoir, and the third and easiest is toward the center of the rock mass.

The Wine Glass

DESCRIPTION

This elongated ridge of picturesque slickrock domes and terraces offers a relatively small but easily accessible multi-level area of hiking that provides splendid panoramic views from its upper reaches of the Hatch Point rimlands and the colorful canyon country beyond. Some of the slickrock slopes that grant passage between the sandstone domes in the center of the ridge are so steep that they should be avoided by less experienced slickrock hikers, but this still leaves a considerable area and several levels to explore.

Only hikers with free-climbing skills and experience should attempt to reach the summit of Flat Iron Mesa, the high sandstone butte that dominates the northern end of this slickrock ridge.

Like so many such flat-topped Navajo Sandstone domes in the general Hatch Point vicinity, the truncated summit of this mesa was formed by the high erosion resistance of petrified, highly-mineralized sediments that were originally deposited within a vast region of desert dunes as ephemeral pools, or desert dry-lakes. Geologists call such shallow, temporary desert lakes "playas." The rock strata found in "petrified playas" are generally light gray in color.

A few such desert lakes were spring-fed and hence lasted long enough to host shrubs, trees and even animal life. "Petrified oases" sediments are usually darker colored than those of playas, and sometimes contain petrified wood and animal tracks.

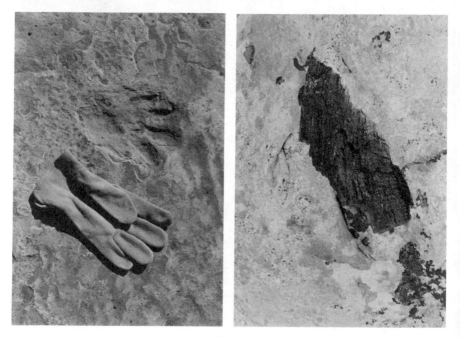

Hatch Point Lowlands

NAME - HATCH POINT LOWLANDS

TYPE - area

ROCK - Cutler Group and Cutler-Cedar Mesa Sandstone undivided

USE - hiking and biking

GUIDEBOOK & MAP - *Canyon Country* OFF-ROAD VEHICLE TRAILS - **Canyon Rims & Needles Areas** and matching map

VEHICLE - off-road vehicle

ACCESS

Drive the Lockhart Basin ORV trail from either end, as described in the referenced book and map. This trail spurs from the Chicken Corners trail at its north end, and from paved Utah 211 in the south.

From the north, drive this ORV trail until it is traveling the benchlands near the western cliffs of lofty Hatch Point.

From the south, drive this trail for a mile or so beyond where it fords lower Indian Creek in a colorful redrock canyon.

DESCRIPTION

The Lockhart Basin ORV trail skirts the base of Hatch Point for many miles between its north end and just north of the broad mouth of Harts Draw, an immense drainage that joins lower Indian Creek. Between the two points noted in ACCESS, the terrain to the west of this trail is undivided Cutler sandstone in the north, and undivided Cutler-Cedar Mesa sandstone in the south. These formations are quite colorful and closely resemble each other. Their inconspicuous interface is about 1/2 mile north of where the trail crosses the main drainage of Rustler Canyon. Both formations make excellent hiking, and highly challenging mountain biking is possible in many stretches.

Hiking and biking possibilities begin within a mile or so of where the trail spurs south from the Chicken Corners trail, and continue until the trail descends into the softer sediments of Lockhart Basin. They resume when the trail again travels fairly close to the base of Hatch Point, and continue on south to lower Indian Creek Canyon.

Traveling the trail from the south, the best slickrock hiking to the west of the trail begins shortly after the trail climbs out of lower Indian Creek Canyon, continues to the softer sediments of Lockhart Basin, then resumes beyond the basin.

Hikers and bikers should choose areas to explore along this long, convoluted stretch of highly eroded slickrock that appeal to their sense of esthetics or challenge, as the case may be. Almost any part of this area makes excellent hiking, with many square miles of broken, canyon-carved rock available from any part of the trail.

Bikers will need to be more selective, but will still find large areas that can be biked with close attention to navigation, although it will be necessary to travel short stretches of softer material between slick-rock expanses in many places, and ledging will require bicycle transporting for short distances.

Altogether, this stretch of slickrock is one of the most colorful and scenic to be found in the canyon country region, and it offers unusual variety and novelty in erosional forms. The setting is outstanding, with the looming cliffs of Hatch Point to the east, the meandering Colorado River gorge far below, and with the soaring plateau of Island-in-the-Sky in Canyonlands National Park dominating the western skyline. From some areas the redrock spires of the Needles are visible to the south.

NAME - PRITCHETT - HUNTER MESA

TYPE - area

ROCK - Navajo Sandstone

USE - hiking only

GUIDEBOOK & MAP - *Canyon Country* OFF-ROAD VEHICLE TRAILS - Canyon Rims & Needles Areas and matching map

VEHICLE - highway vehicle one access, off-road vehicle otherwise

ACCESS

Drive downriver from Moab on Cane Creek Road, as described in the referenced book and map, to where the road has ascended high above the narrows of lower Cane Creek Canyon and is about to descend back into the canyon via some steep switchback curves. Park at a pull-out near the top of this grade, where a small tributary drainage has cut an alcove in the Navajo Sandstone above and to the left of the road. This is the only access point to Pritchett-Hunter Mesa that can be reached by highway vehicles.

To reach one of the two other practical access points, drive up Pritchett Canyon from Cane Creek Road on the Pritchett Canyon-Behind the Rocks ORV trail, as described in the referenced book and map, to the spur trail near the head of Pritchett Canyon that approaches Halls Bridge.

For an easier but longer access approach, drive the Cane Creek Canyon Rim ORV trail from its southern end into the upper Hunter Canyon drainage, then park at the head of the hiking trail to Pritchett Arch.

DESCRIPTION

Pritchett-Hunter Mesa is an elevated, irregular mesa about 2-1/2 miles long and 1-1/4 miles wide that is entirely Navajo Sandstone except for some areas of loose, sandy soils. The mesa is defined by Pritchett Canyon, the upper and lower Hunter Canyon drainage, lower Cane Creek Canyon and a bit of the Colorado River gorge. The mesa is isolated by sheer sandstone cliffs except for three practical access points. The access point from Cane Creek Road is the easiest to reach by vehicle, but involves the most risky climb onto the mesa. Some hikers may prefer the other routes.

From the first access point described, hike and climb up the steep drainage indicated onto an intermediate terrace high above the road and find lovely Funnel Arch. Beyond the arch, it is possible to climb up the sloping edge of a large slickrock fin, then on up to the top of this elevated mesa.

The route to Funnel Arch

The first access point from the Pritchett Canyon-Behind the Rocks ORV trail is from the end of the short spur trail to Halls Bridge. The hiking route up onto the mesa behind and above this picturesque natural arch begins at the end of the spur vehicle trail. Hike up to the rocky, sandy slopes below the arch, then continue hiking up the narrow drainage below the arch to the top of the mesa. From there, it is possible to hike around the slickrock fins and back down to the opening through Halls Bridge, or across its top.

Ascending Halls Bridge

Funnel Arch

From this access point, exploring the immense, elevated slickrock mesa is strictly freestyle, but the most scenic routes travel as close as practical to the mesa rimlands, which offer breathtaking views down into the canyons that form the mesa, and beyond them into the massive Navajo Sandstone labyrinth of Behind the Rocks, or across Hunter Canyon to the tilted Cane Creek Canyon rimlands.

The third access point is from the upper Hunter Canyon drainage. To reach it, drive on up Pritchett Canyon and over its summit, then descend into the lower terrain beyond. About 1 mile beyond the canyon summit, turn right on the short spur trail that ends at the hiking trailhead to beautiful Pritchett Arch.

As an alternate to driving the rough and steep ORV trail up Pritchett Canyon, the trailhead to Pritchett Arch can also be reached by driving the Cane Creek Canyon Rim ORV trail from U.S. 191, as described in the referenced book and map, then driving down the short connecting trail into the upper Hunter Canyon drainage and up that to the Pritchett Arch spur trail.

From the parking area, hike to Pritchett Arch. It is possible to climb up onto Pritchett-Hunter Mesa by hiking beyond the arch, where there are spectacular views down into upper Pritchett Canyon, then climbing up a steep sandstone slope about 1/4 mile beyond the span. This route is somewhat risky.

For a safer route up, go back to where the foot trail to the arch first reaches the top of the cliff that looms above the parking area, then hike left, or clockwise, around the high sandstone domes to anywhere that it is fairly easy to climb upward into the sandstone maze above Pritchett Arch. Some hikers might enjoy returning to the arch and walking out onto this wide span, or onto the narrower ridge behind it.

From this access point it is again a matter of freelance hiking, with the mesa rimlands offering the best views. The mesa is so immense that several days can easily be spent exploring its intricacies and enjoying its spectacular scenic views. Hikers who arrange for transportation, can ascend the mesa at Pritchett Arch, visit Halls Bridge, explore the mesa for a day or two, then descend via Funnel Arch, or reverse this route.

On top of Pritchett Arch

NAME - CANE CREEK CANYON RIMLANDS

TYPE - area

ROCK - Wingate and Kayenta sandstones

USE - hiking and limited biking

GUIDEBOOK & MAP - *Canyon Country* OFF-ROAD VEHICLE TRAILS - Canyon Rims & Needles Areas and matching map

VEHICLE - off-road vehicle

ACCESS

Drive to the end of the Cane Creek Canyon Rim ORV trail from U.S. 191 as described in the referenced book and map. Be sure to stay on the relatively obscure stretch of this trail that continues closely parallel to the canyon rim beyond where the more obvious route descends steeply toward the east. The Cane Creek Canyon Rim trail continues for more than 2 miles beyond this inconspicuous junction, and stays quite close to the rim all the way. Park anywhere along the last mile or two of the trail and hike from there.

DESCRIPTION

This large area of steeply sloping sandstone is unusual in two ways. It is the western rim of an immense syncline, or gigantic sag in the surface rock strata. Water draining into the lower part of this syncline formed both Hunter and Pritchett canyons.

This area is another of the few places where the top of the cliff-forming Wingate Sandstone is exposed to a considerable extent. About half of this area is the top of the Wingate, with remnants of the ledgy Kayenta sandstone still lying on the rest of it. In most areas, the hard Kayenta strata protect the top of the Wingate, but here the extreme slope created by the syncline has accelerated removal of the Kayenta by allowing rapid water runoff to undercut it.

This area is defined by Cane Creek Canyon on two sides, the Hunter Canyon drainage on another, and the ORV trail that descends into the syncline valley on the fourth side.

As the ORV trail continues along the rim of Cane Creek Canyon beyond the descending spur trail, it enters an area that has been disturbed by bulldozing and drilling. This was done to trace the ore veins being sought in the uranium mines at the base of the cliff. The damage has since largely been reclaimed by erosion, but it still obscures the trail in several places. The vehicle trail ends at a point almost directly opposite Hurrah Pass, the saddle in the opposite rim of Cane Creek Canyon that is below lofty Anticline Overlook, a developed viewpoint in the Canyon Rims Recreation Area.

From anywhere near the end of the vehicle trail, hikers and bikers can chose their routes. The high rim offers the best views of Cane Creek Canyon, Hurrah Pass, the Colorado River gorge beyond and the elevated peninsulas of Dead Horse Point and Island-in-the-Sky on the western skyline.

Below the canyon rim, hiking becomes more challenging, and biking more difficult, as minor drainages on the rim become deeper farther down the syncline slope. Eventually these drainages join to become the deep and lovely Hunter Canyon drainage, but above that lower limit there are several square miles of excellent slickrock hiking and biking, with outstanding views down into and across the syncline toward the Behind the Rocks maze, the Moab Rim and the distant La Sal Mountains.

Altogether, this slickrock area presents splendidly varied canyon country hiking, biking and viewing, across terrain that has been tortured by stupendous geologic forces for millions of years, then left to erode into a labyrinth of sandstone canyons, domes, valleys and sheer-walled fins.

NAME - CASA COLORADO

TYPE - area

ROCK - Entrada-Slickrock member

USE - hiking and biking

GUIDEBOOK & MAP - Utah Travel Council map of Southeastern Utah

VEHICLE - highway vehicle

ACCESS

Drive east from U.S. 191 on paved San Juan County Road 114, as shown on the referenced map. This junction is about 5-1/2 miles south of Wilson Arch on U.S. 191, or about 2-1/2 miles north of the paved entrance road into Canyon Rims Recreation Area. Drive east for about 4-1/2 miles on Road 114, to the east end of the immense sandstone mass called Casa Colorado. Park off the road and hike or bike around the eastern end of Casa Colorado for a short distance on the ORV trail there. Before the drainage that develops along the base of the cliff becomes too deep to cross easily, cross it and continue around the base of the cliff onto the eroded slopes that drain south from this elongated, colorful slickrock butte.

Casa Colorado

DESCRIPTION

This relatively small but colorful and historic slickrock area can be sampled in a half-day of freelance exploring, but a more detailed exploration of all the area has to offer requires a full day.

Casa Colorado (Red House) was named by early Spanish explorers because to them the domed "roof" and several arching alcoves on the south face of the eastern end of the long rock mass resembled a gigantic house. A reliable water source just south of Casa Colorado was named "La Tinaja," or "The Tank," and was on the historic route through this region now called the "Old Spanish Trail." The location and name of La Tinaja was known to, and the water was used by, the 1859 Macomb expedition, the first American party to venture into what is now southeastern Utah.

La Tinaja, Old Spanish Trail waterhole

Unlike many early Spanish geographic names, "Casa Colorado" survived into the present and appears on U.S. Geological Survey maps, together with other such names as the Abajo and La Sal mountains, and the San Juan and Colorado rivers. But the location and name of the water hole "La Tinaja" was lost to history until relocated and identified in the late 1980s.

For more about this rediscovery and the 1859 Macomb expedition, refer to the books, **CANYONLANDS NATIONAL PARK** - *Early History & First Descriptions* and **HIKING THE HISTORIC ROUTE of the 1859 MACOMB EXPEDITION.** The latter book can be useful in exploring this slickrock area.

Once on the slickrock slopes south of Casa Colorado, the hiking and biking is freelance, with no particular route. The easternmost drainage line soon develops broad slickrock terraces on one side that are littered with interesting mineral specimens, and eventually cascades down a slickrock drop to join the central drainage. A few hundred feet on down this joint drainage, a small but graceful natural bridge on the left spans the lower end of an adjoining slickrock area, with a small water catchment that makes delightful contrast with the red-hued sandstone when full.

From its confluence with the eastern drainage line, the central drainage ascends potholed slickrock with sandy stretches, to reach an undercut pouroff from the higher, more hikable slickrock. The La Tinaja water hole is just above this pouroff, as a deep, cylindrical hole in the solid rock of the main drainage. This natural tank can hold more than 2,000 gallons of water, and always contains some water even after months of desert drought.

To explore further from here, hike on up the drainage toward Casa Colorado then, from near its base, continue westward around the immense amphitheater toward the relatively low arm of colorful Entrada sandstone that protrudes southward from the higher butte. Hike up this arm as far as feasible on both sides of the butte. This promontory offers an excellent panoramic view of the many outstanding geologic features toward the south and west. The 1859 Macomb expedition came through the gap between the cliffline directly to the south and the detached white sandstone domes a bit west, heading toward La Tinaja, where the expedition camped before heading for the next water hole on the Old Spanish Trail, in their search for the fabled confluence of the Green and Grand (Colorado) rivers, which were then still unmapped in this general region.

Baird Bridge, near Casa Colorado

119

A MID-WINTER ADVENTURE

Bartlett Wash is a broad, V-shaped canyon with beautiful red-rock walls. These walls are more than two miles apart at the upper end of the canyon, but are barely a few hundred feet apart in its lower end. The south wall is continuous, unbroken in its entire length, although as sinuous in contour as a great serpent.

The north wall, however, while it appears to the casual glance to be continuous, is not. An obscure gap in the wall gives a tantalizing glimpse into a tributary canyon that we long ago dubbed "Hidden Canyon" -- because it is.

Hidden Canyon is a glorious labyrinth of beautifully eroded Entrada slickrock walls, intruding fins and peninsulas, luring side-canyons and sandy washes, all rimmed by remnants of the white Entrada Moab member and still higher Morrison deposits.

An ORV trail reaches its northern rim, and two very chancy trails enter the canyon bottom, one through the inconspicuous portal into Bartlett, the other through an obscure second drainage. Neither trail sees much use, one because of its extremely sandy nature, the other because it is almost impossible to get back up the sand-hill that must be descended to get to the portal.

Even so, we had driven into Hidden Canyon many times, by both routes, and had explored its maze-like drainage system on foot. We had also visited its two overlooking viewpoints, one on the northern rim, the other high on a Morrison mesa to the west.

But we had never found a way to get up onto the beautiful slickrock mid-level of Hidden Canyon that was as alluring to us as a shady-green oasis to a sun-weary dune-desert traveler. For years we had sought a way down from above, without having to use climbing ropes and skills, and from below, in the labyrinthine canyon itself. It was one of my major frustrations, seeing from above that brilliantly colorful, elevated-maze of slickrock terraces and benches and ledges and jutting peninsulas, but not being able to set foot on it. Then we had some luck, in the form of a young friend who is even more adventurous than we are.

We had taken this friend on some of our favorite slickrock hiking routes in the Bartlett Wash area, and had then left him camping out in a cottonwood grove just below the canyon narrows, after telling him of our frustrations with Hidden Canyon, and challenging him to find a way up onto that elusive mid-level.

Two days later, he returned to tell us of his subsequent hikes -- and of having found a way up into that slickrock paradise. He described the route he had found and marked a map for us, showing its probable location. He wasn't absolutely sure.

He also mentioned having stayed up there so long exploring that his trip back down was almost a disaster. In the gathering dusk, he had been unable to find the inconspicuous route, and had fruitlessly explored several large sandstone peninsulas before finally finding and descending the hazardous route in the dark, aided only by a tiny flashlight fastened to a headband.

Time passed -- a couple of months or more. It was autumn, and the best time to explore canyon country, so, as usual, we made the most of it. Despite my strong desire to try for our friend's route up in Hidden Canyon, it was mid-winter before we finally got around to checking it out.

On the first day of January, a beautiful, calm, clear but cold day, we set out just to see if we could find that route, but certainly not to "go for it." On New Year's Day? Mid-winter?" With the temperature in the 20s? Of course not -- but we took along lunch anyway, because we still expected to spend the entire lovely, typical-canyon-country-winter-day exploring -- in our heated Land Cruiser.

Since it was the shortest way into Hidden Canyon, we drove toward its portal and paused at the head of the horrendous sandhill that was not negotiable most of the year. I scrambled and slid down the badly eroded trail to the wash bottom, then looked back up. I felt sure I could handle the eroded ruts, but there was a final three-foot drop that was almost vertical, where transient flooding had cut into the base of the entire sandhill.

Impossible -- if the sand was not moist and frozen solid, which it was. I decided to take a chance. From where we were parked, it was still too long a hike into Hidden Canyon for that time of the year. Besides, if I couldn't get back up the sandhill, we could leave the canyon by the other route -- I hoped.

I climbed back up the steep trail, got into the vehicle, we buckled in tightly and headed down the trail. The descent was more or less a controlled fall, a sandy slide to the bottom, with just enough steering to keep the wheels out of the deeply eroded ruts, then down that final three-foot drop into the wash, where the front bumper dug into the wash-bottom and the rear bumper rounded off the sandy ledge.

The drive on into the canyon was routine, although most of the way I had my head stuck out of the window, trying to orient the terrain to our friend's marked map. That was not easy, especially from our wash-bottom viewpoint, like mice in a maze. As they say, "the map is not the territory." Amen to that!

121

On up the main wash, we finally paused for a stretch and a look around, parking beside a long, rounded slickrock fin that I thought looked like a way up, even though there was a distant ledge on up the route that would probably bar the way. I hiked on ahead along the base of the fin, seeking a way up. My wife tagged leisurely along behind, admiring the intricate erosion patterns in the walls of the fin. There was very little snow anywhere, but shaded ledges had ice here and there, remnants of sun-melted snow that had refrozen as it dripped down the rock into the shade, and of frozen seep-water in tiny alcoves.

I finally found a chancy way up, but called down asking my wife to wait until I had explored on ahead to see if the ledge I had seen would be surmountable. Meantime, she explored the fin in the other direction and, by the time I got back with the news that the route might be feasible, she had found an easier way up to my level. We walked on up to the ledge for a closer look.

Eager to try the climb, I started up. A shrub blocked the way near the top, but I managed anyway, then set out to see if the way on was clear of hazards. It was, so I called back down, asking my wife to go back to the vehicle, put our lunches, a climbing rope and my camera into the day-pack we always carried with us, and come back to the hazardous ledge.

She did, and on her return managed to throw one rope-end up to me, after several tries. I then used it to pull up the pack, and to help her safely up the ledge. We then went on up the gigantic red-slickrock fin, jubilant over our success at finding a way up -- perhaps the one our friend had described, perhaps not -- and eager to continue our crazy mid-winter adventure.

The sandstone level we had reached was lovely, breathtaking, spectacular, glorious, colorful -- the English language is simply not capable of describing canyon country at its best -- not enough adjectives for the myriad forms of esthetic beauty here.

The rest of the short winter morning went quickly, as we explored the flat top and each intermediate level and colorful terrace and secret alcove of each sandstone peninsula that jutted into the complex canyon. We had a bit of trouble getting on to the final gigantic fin that separated Hidden Canyon from the main gorge of Bartlett Wash. To avoid walking along a very narrow ledge above a deadly drop, we had climbed to the base of the higher Entrada Moab member wall and skirted close to that, even though that route was made difficult by brush, trees, fallen rock and steep sandy-soil slopes.

Once on top of that great dividing wall, we headed toward where we knew the Hidden Canyon portal had to be, seeking a special place for lunch. We soon found it, at the base of a low, smoothly eroded redrock ledge, facing the warm winter sun -- and overlooking an immense slick-rock pothole full of frozen water, an ice-pond some thirty by fifteen feet in size. A tossed rock just bounced and skidded along the surface of the pond.

Beyond our miniature ice-skating rink, in its setting of rounded red slickrock, the whole lower end of Bartlett Wash was in view, with the snow-capped peaks of the La Sals looming above the distant south wall of the huge canyon. It was truly a spectacular and unique place to enjoy our New Year's Day lunch.

After relishing our portable meal of sandwiches, cookies and hot tea, we continued our explorations, enjoying every endlessly varied view of the intricately eroded slickrock labyrinth, gasping at the drops at the end of each gigantic salmon-hued fin, and continually marveling at the myriad shapes that Entrada slickrock can take when eroded and weath-ered for millennia in an arid high-desert environment. And also working off years of frustration over not being able to find a way up into this esthetic oasis, this ultimate slickrock-paradise hiking area.

As the short winter day waned, we reluctantly headed back toward our vehicle, retracing our difficult route along the base of the higher wall. And there, where we had missed them earlier, we found foot tracks! There was only one set of them, so we concluded they were our friend's, still there months after being made in the soft, sandy soil, and the only traces of humanity we had seen all day long. Yet one of the reasons why the government had rejected this area for wilderness con-sideration had been because it offered "no chance for a wilderness expe-rience." Insane!

Back at the head of the ascent route, we used the climbing rope to help my wife safely down, and to lower the pack to her, but with nothing on the bare slickrock to loop around for a rappel down, I had to descend unaided, a task I did not enjoy. While catching my breath at the base of the ledge, I vowed next time to bring the tools needed to place an anchor bolt above the ledge, where I could catch it with a loop from below, and use it for the climb up and a rappel descent. So far, I have not done this.

At our vehicle, tired, a little chilled by the lack of sunlight in the canyon-bottom in late afternoon, and a bit concerned about getting back up that sand-ledge, we loaded up and headed back for that "moment-of-truth." Would the rounding off of that sandy ledge by the vehicle on its sliding descent make the climb back up easier? Time would tell.

After following the twisting wash-bottom path between the looming, shadowed walls of Hidden Canyon's portal, we reached the base of the trail back up. Had the day's sunlight warmed the sandhill so that it would be less solidly frozen?

I set the vehicle in its lowest gear, said *"hang on,"* and without further hesitation headed for the sandy ledge. And up we went, with the engine growling and all four big, deep-tread tires clawing away at the steep, sandy trail, while I fought to keep the wheels from sliding sideways into the deep erosion ruts and trapping us -- some seven miles from the nearest road, and at dusk in the dead of winter.

Although that climb lasted only a few seconds, it seemed like eternity before we finally topped out and we could breath again. With this one last hazard conquered, we then headed home, enthusing all the way back about the spectacularly successful day we had experienced, the great start we had made in a new year, still riding the buoyant feeling of having overcome a series of daunting obstacles, of having thoroughly erased a long-standing set of frustrations. It was a great New Year, indeed!

Later ---

124

ISLAND AREA

This geographic area is defined by Interstate 70 in the north, U.S. 191 and the Colorado river in the east, and the Green River in the west. The perimeter highways and the roads and off-road vehicle trails within the area are described in another *Canyon Country* guidebook and matching map. These are listed by title in each area description and on the inside-back cover of this book.

NAME - ARTHS RIM

TYPE - area

ROCK - Kayenta and Wingate sandstones

USE - hiking and biking

GUIDEBOOK & MAP - *Canyon Country* OFF-ROAD VEHICLE TRAILS - Island Area and matching map

VEHICLE - off-road vehicle

ACCESS

Drive west and south on Utah 313 from U.S. 191, then east on the graded dirt Arths Pasture Road to its junction with the Sevenmile Canyon Rim ORV trail. The route to this point is passable to highway vehicles, although the dirt road may be rough. Angle left on the ORV trail.

There are two distinct areas of hikable slickrock in the Arths Rim area. Only one of these offers much off-trail biking.

The last mile of the Sevenmile Canyon Rim ORV trail, along elevated Arths Rim, provides access to the higher of these two areas. Two inconspicuous spurs from the same trail provide access to the other area, one to its lower reaches and the other directly into the heart of the best hiking and biking. The lower access route is less practical for bikers because access to the slickrock area is up steep sandstone slopes and ledges.

DESCRIPTION

    To explore the upper slickrock rimlands of Arths Rim, drive or bike to the end of the Sevenmile Canyon Rims trail and park. This area can be explored on foot various places along the last mile or more of the trail, but the best hiking area is along the rimlands of Little Canyon beyond the end of the ORV trail.

    A highlight in this area is massive Lynn-Lin Arch, a picturesque span that is between two of the many "hanging canyons" that are down-rim from the end of the ORV trail. Since there is no practical way to describe how to find this well-hidden arch, hikers will have the pleasure of finding it on their own, from just knowing that it is within about 1/4 mile of the ORV trail-end, at a lower elevation, and visible in the slick-rock fins in the rim high above, from one short stretch of the ORV trail that travels the narrows of Little Canyon.

Lin-Lynn Arch

127

To reach the lower approach to the second and lower slickrock area of Arths Rim that is both hikable and bikable, watch for an inconspicuous spur that goes right from the Sevenmile Canyon Rim trail about 3-1/2 miles from the trail start. This spur goes under some power lines within a few yards, then descends into terrain broken by a series of drainages through terraced, ledgy Kayenta sandstone.

About 3/4 mile from the trail junction, take the left trail spur that crosses a small exposure of slickrock. Shortly beyond this inconspicuous trail junction, the ORV trail passes an easy route on the right up a sloping slickrock ledge that goes toward the lower hikable canyon rims area. Where this trail ends shortly in a canyon, in view of a large arch, more adventurous hikers can ascend the canyon wall opposite the arch by climbing a series of slickrock ledges and slopes toward, then beyond, a large conspicuous boulder balanced high on the canyon rim.

After ascending the ledges behind the balanced rock, continue up the canyon rim to the rimlands that skirt the several major canyons that drain the higher elevations of Arths Rim. The hiking above these canyons, and along the sloping slickrock peninsulas that separate them, offers many outstanding views into the picturesque canyons and across Arths Pasture toward the complex drainages of the Bull and Sevenmile canyon systems.

To reach this hikable-bikable lower area of slickrock directly, drive about 3-3/4 miles from the start of the Sevenmile Canyon Rim ORV trail to the spur that descends left to the lower rimlands of Sevenmile Canyon. Continue ahead to where the trail goes beneath some power lines, then watch for an inconspicuous spur that goes right from this trail just before it starts a steep and rough climb. Go right on this rough spur trail for a few hundred yards, until it reaches the first expanses of slickrock and park anywhere convenient. Start hiking or biking from there, in a southeasterly direction, across the heads of the lower canyons described earlier, exploring down into and between the canyons at various levels.

These strangely sloping canyons and the slickrock expanses that surround them offer several days of delightful and demanding slickrock exploration for hikers. Bikers will need at least one full day to explore the area that is bikable. Hikers with climbing skills and equipment may find exploring some of the narrow and steep slots at the heads of these canyons enjoyable.

NAME - BARTLETT NORTH RIM

TYPE - route

ROCK - Entrada-Slickrock member

USE - hiking and limited biking

GUIDEBOOK & MAP - *Canyon Country* OFF-ROAD VEHICLE TRAILS - Island Area and matching map

VEHICLE - highway vehicle

ACCESS

Drive north from Moab on U.S. 191, west on Utah 313, then north on the Dubinky Well Road, as described in the referenced book and map. About 4 miles north of where this road leaves Utah 313, watch for a fenceline, with an ORV trail going right a few yards beyond the fence. Drive or walk this trail for about 1/4 mile to a gate in the fence. The slickrock north rim of Bartlett Wash begins a few yards beyond this gate.

DESCRIPTION

Hike along the fenceline as it continues beyond the gate then angles south toward the red sandstone rim, which is the interface between the Dewey Bridge and Slickrock members of Entrada sandstone. The rim is above a large amphitheater of barren red and white rock and sediments, and is set with dark red, weather-rounded balanced rocks and "goblins." There are numerous specimens of chert and Dewey Bridge agate along the rim.

Continue along the rim, which soon becomes a terrace just below the higher Entrada-Slickrock member, as far as practical, which is about 30 yards beyond a long stretch of deeply undercut Entrada-Slickrock. For hiking variety, stay on the colorful weather-sculpted higher level on the return trip.

Bikers should avoid this lower approach, and will find that the first 3/4 mile of the higher slickrock terrace makes an excellent multi-level "gymnasium," but should not continue along the rim beyond the huge alcove near the base of the high butte of younger deposits, and should avoid making wheel tracks in the softer sediments and soils in the main slickrock terrace. The best way to explore farther along the rim is by hiking.

The western end of this spectacular rim is very little elevated above the wash, but soon turns into broad terraces of solid slickrock that become steadily higher above the terrain to the south. The sandstones in this area provide lovely examples of red and white interlayering, both from wind and water.

131

As the main slickrock terrace approaches the high promontory of newer deposits, and the cliffline below the hiking route becomes broken by protruding fins, watch for two small windows in one such immense sandstone abutment, about 3/4 mile from the gate where the hike begins. In this vicinity, it is worth exploring the several levels of eroded, red and white slickrock, and the large crevices and terraces that separate them.

Not far beyond this area, a major drainage must be passed, either by walking a narrow, sloping ledge above a sheer drop, or by bypassing it at a higher level, then dropping down from a ledge. Just beyond this hazard, several complex drainage lines have cut small but lovely canyons back into the solid sandstone that are worth exploring.

Beyond these canyons, a complex, multi-level promontory is also worth exploring in detail. It sometimes has potholes full of water, and exhibits beautiful variety in color and shape of the already colorful slickrock. The broad, lofty terrace that continues down the canyon rim is liberally sprinkled with curious mineral specimens, and along the base of the still higher wall of Moab Member Entrada sandstone, pinyon, juniper and other trees and desert shrubs grow in sandy soils and fallen rock debris. Hikers should take special care to avoid walking on the extensive cryptogamic soils along this rimland route, because they add to the natural beauty of this lofty, linear ecosystem.

Bartlett North Rim, looking east

After a short distance, it is once again possible to hike along levels of slickrock somewhat lower than the top terrace. In this stretch, a long, open crevice parallel to the cliff edge is the narrow opening of lofty Bartlett Bridge, which is visible in the high north wall of Bartlett Wash from the Dubinky Well Road that is used for access to this hiking route.

Farther along the rim, broad lower terraces and jutting peninsulas of slickrock are well worth exploring, then the upper terrace narrows, cut by drainage lines that are topped by immense, arch-roofed alcoves in the white upper wall of sandstone. This upper layer is Entrada-Moab member sandstone.

One of these large alcoves marks the practical end of safe hiking along this route. Skilled climbers who are not troubled by sheer drops may be able to continue beyond this drainage, but this is not recommended for the average hiker. Another route along this same rim that begins in Hidden Canyon approaches this hazardous drainage from the other direction.

Bartlett North Rim, from above

BIOTURBATION

The western end of the north rim of Bartlett Wash is one of our favorite slickrock hiking areas. All three colorful members of Entrada Sandstone are there, and each makes up part of the long, convoluted canyon wall.

The top of the entire miles-long northern cliffline is fairly level, but the canyon floor below it drops away, leaving the canyon walls in its central section quite high.

At its western end, the wall fades inconspicuously into the surrounding terrain -- broad, sandy blackbrush meadows, set with low slickrock exposures and higher domes and ridges of Navajo Sandstone. The softer Dewey Bridge member there forms a broad, colorful basin set with low "goblins" of eroded, dark-red rock.

As we started our hike along the westernmost stretch of rim, we stayed as close to the edge as feasible, so as to enjoy the myriad fantastic shapes weathered into the Dewey Bridge sandstone, in both the amphitheater below and along the base of the cliff. This soon became a broad terrace, at an intermediate level between the red-hued terrain below and the harder, more uniform sandstone strata of the Slickrock member above us. The interface between the two members was deeply undercut in places, making interesting alcoves and caves to explore.

Then we reached a practical end to the terrace. We could continue along it only at considerable risk of a deadly fall. Being safety-conscious by nature -- this is essential if you want to survive long in this hazard-filled land -- we chose to climb up a nearby rockfall to the next higher level, the lowest terrace in the Slickrock member.

There, we continued slowly, marveling at the strangely beautiful colors and erosional shapes of the white and red slickrock. The rock was layered, with most distinct horizontal layers exhibiting the sharply-sloping cross-stratification typical in sand-dune deposits, but with each layer several feet thick being separated by a thin, level water-affected layer. We mused about this odd combination.

Was the paleoenvironment perhaps a low, arid coastal plain subject to occasional tidal invasions? Geology books say nothing about such oddities. They tend to deal with larger, more obvious phenomena. Another of the myriad mysteries of this ancient land.

We also observed places where there was distinct dune-sand cross-stratification, but with alternating laminations being red and white. This defied one geologic theory about the rock colors in this region, the one that held that none of the redrock strata here were red when first deposited -- that they turned red over eons, megayears, as the result of underground chemical reactions involving exceptionally high atmospheric oxygen, ground water and iron-bearing mineral granules that were not red when deposited.

This, and other field evidence we had observed, meant that this scientific hypothesis did not explain as much as the geologists thought. There was more to it. Some sediments were *already* red when deposited, with no subsequent chemical reactions.

Then we came to another strange phenomenon, one we had never seen before. A layer of grayish sandstone four feet thick, separated from more typical reddish strata above and below by a thin water-affected layer, had a series of strange ridges in it, where its gently sloping surface was exposed by erosion.

On closer examination, we could see a pattern. The tops of all the ridges were much darker, harder rock, and thus more resistant to surface weathering. Some were low, just an inch or so higher than the base rock. Others were as high as two feet, with a roughly-cylindrical tube of the harder rock supported on a sinuous wall of the softer gray rock. The sloping cylinders of harder rock were serving as linear cap-rocks, protecting the softer stone below from rain-erosion -- the same mechanism that forms so many balanced rocks.

Along the curving line of this odd deposit there were dozens, perhaps hundreds of these twisting, angled, hardrock cylinders, some lying low against the surface, others perched on elevated supports. Each began and ended at the interface with the next layer above or below. A few, with the upper halves of their cylinders removed by erosion, indicated that at one time material from the red layer above had seeped down through holes in their centers -- like red sediments flowing down a tube?

After considerable thoughtful observation and discussion, we were forced to conclude that the strange angled tubes were not natural -- they were not a geologic phenomenon. They had to have been made by some kind of life. Plant roots? That didn't fit. They were almost all the same size, and in some cases intersected and crossed each other, with larger cylinders where they met -- like tunnels widened for more convenient passing?

Passing? That sounded like animal burrows! That idea fit almost everything we could see, except one -- all the "burrows" slanted downward from what had then been the surface at about the same angle. How could *that* be explained?

Well, conventional geologists and paleontologists have a way of getting around such mysteries. They hang a descriptive term on them, then go on to other subjects. They would call these odd phenomena we had discovered "bioturbation," meaning some kind of disturbance of fresh deposits by some kind of life.

So we had found evidence of bioturbation -- big deal! But what caused it? That's what we wanted to know -- and still do. Is there anyone out there who can offer an explanation?

135

NAME - BARTLETT - HIDDEN CANYON RIMS

TYPE - area and route

ROCK - Entrada-Slickrock member

USE - hiking and limited biking

GUIDEBOOK & MAP - *Canyon Country* OFF-ROAD VEHICLE
TRAILS - Island Area and matching map

VEHICLE - off-road vehicle

ACCESS

   Drive north from Moab on U.S. 191, west on the Blue Hills Road
then south on the Bartlett Wash ORV trail, as described in the referenced book and map. Beyond the spring-wet narrows in lower Bartlett
Wash, continue upcanyon on the mapped trail for about 1-1/2 miles, to a
trail spur to the right across dune-sand, just beyond where the main trail
climbs onto higher ground and levels off. From this junction, Hidden
Canyon is visible through a gap in the nearby cliff wall. Drive or walk the
spur trail to where it begins to descend into the Hidden Canyon drainage. Vehicles should not be taken down this steep and sandy spur and
on up the wash bottom into Hidden Canyon without first making certain
that the vehicle used can return by the same route.

Hidden Canyon

136

There is an alternate way out of this box-canyon, but some stretches of that trail are also very eroded and sandy. The safest way to enter and explore the Hidden Canyon slickrock area and the Bartlett Wash rimlands beyond is on foot, from at or near the described trail junction, or by hiking all the way up into Hidden Canyon from where its narrow and picturesque lower drainage joins the main Bartlett Wash drainage.

A second slickrock route and area that can be explored from the lower Bartlett Wash narrows begins at the spring-wet narrows.

DESCRIPTION

Exploring every part of the slickrock-and-sand maze of Hidden Canyon can take days, and is a beautiful and rewarding experience, but most of this description is limited to telling how to attain the tops of the several gigantic red sandstone peninsulas that jut into the canyon from the west and southwest, how to explore them, then continue along the same level of the North Rim of Bartlett Wash to the alcove that blocked progress along the westernmost stretch of the rim, as described in the Bartlett North Rim route. The first area and route described is for hikers only.

After entering Hidden Canyon, hike up the main wash for about 3/4 mile beyond the canyon portal. At this point, there is a long, relatively low peninsula of slickrock to the left of the wash, with a partly detached dome of sandstone at its end. Climb up to and through the gap between the peninsula and dome, then up onto the peninsula and toward where it joins the higher levels of rock.

At that point, the route on up is via a rounded terrace and narrow, sloping ledge above that. This is the only way to continue on this route without the use of climbing aids and skills.

Once on the next higher level of this colorful slickrock maze, exploring its intricacies is freestyle, a matter of choice, but for maximum enjoyment of the esthetic aspects of this colorful sandstone it is suggested that each of the several immense slickrock peninsulas that jut out into Hidden Canyon be explored in detail, at every level possible. Photographers will find this elevated, three-dimensional rock maze especially delightful, because of its endless variety of color, shape and lighting.

To reach the high sandstone peninsula that separates Hidden Canyon from Bartlett Wash, it is necessary to walk a narrow ledge of rock above a hazardous drop, or climb to the base of the white higher wall of Moab Member Entrada, then along that wall for some distance before dropping back down. One highlight on this last slickrock peninsula is a very large, elongated pothole on its southeastern flank that generally contains water.

From this lofty wall between spectacular canyons, it is an easy hike on upcanyon along the Bartlett Wash north wall, with outstanding views to the south and west, and down into the broad, cliff-walled canyon all the way.

Hikers are advised to exercise great care in returning to the floor of Hidden Canyon by the route described, or in continuing along the Bartlett north wall route beyond the dangerous alcove. This area is far from help and its ORV trails are not heavily traveled. Hiking alone is not advised, and hikers skilled in the use of climbing rope will find a short length useful at the critical ascent-descent point in Hidden Canyon.

The second slickrock area and route accessible from lower Bartlett Wash begins at the narrows, and can be enjoyed by both hikers and bikers.

Climb up onto the low slickrock slopes to the north of the wash bottom anywhere feasible, then hike or bike the terraced slopes upcanyon toward the portal into Hidden Canyon. Above the portal, there is a large area of complex slickrock worth exploring that can serve as an open playground for bikers. The slickrock slopes that continue down into Hidden Canyon can also be hiked, and biked for some distance. This route can be used by hikers as an alternate way into this beautiful canyon and on toward the area and route described above.

This slickrock area is the least demanding for bikers of the two in lower Bartlett Wash, yet it provides excellent views of the canyon system and complex, inconspicuous Hidden Canyon. Biking the northern rimlands of Hidden Canyon and vicinity is described in another guidebook titled *Canyon Country* **MOUNTAIN BIKING.**

NAME - BARTLETT SOUTH RIM

TYPE - route

ROCK - Entrada-Slickrock member

USE - hiking and limited biking

GUIDEBOOK & MAP - *Canyon Country* **OFF-ROAD VEHICLE TRAILS - Island Area** and matching map

VEHICLE - off-road vehicle

ACCESS

Drive north from Moab on U.S. 191, west on the Blue Hills Road then south on the Bartlett Wash ORV trail, as described in the referenced book and map. Park anywhere convenient just beyond the lower Bartlett Wash spring-wet narrows, near where the first low slickrock terraces appear along the south wall.

DESCRIPTION

This route begins with low, gentle slopes that round off to the canyon floor, but soon its lower slopes end in sheer drops, confining the hikable, bikable area to between the higher wall of white Entrada-Moab member sandstone and the lower sheer drop. Within this broad but sloping band of slickrock, hikers and bikers must seek whatever level seems most feasible for continuing progress. This means changing levels now and then.

For the first mile or so, the slickrock terraces are broad and relatively level, offering bikers a veritable three-dimensional playground, with few lifts or carries required. Then a steep drainage line requires hikers to ascend all the way to the broad shelf that marks the interface between the two Entrada members, even though this level is occasionally awkward to travel because of rock-falls from the higher Moab member. Bikers should not go beyond this steep drainage.

One highlight on the south wall of Bartlett Wash beyond this point is where it closely approaches the upper end of adjacent Tusher Canyon. There, the two canyons come so close to each other that the remaining wall between them is relatively thin, affording excellent views into each canyon system from the lofty slickrock saddle between them. Bikers who wish to reach this outstanding viewpoint should leave their bikes where noted above, then hike the rest of the way.

It is possible to hike beyond this narrows for several miles, on the relatively level terrace that marks the interface between the Slickrock and Moab members of the Entrada, until the wall rounds the wide upper end of Bartlett Wash and continues along the southern rim of the multi-armed mesa of which it is a part. Lofty Skywalk Arch is located in the rim of this mesa, in one of the short canyons that slice into its south-facing wall.

Some of this extended route is on sandy soils and debris from the still-higher wall of Moab Member Entrada. The best way to travel this elevated, twisting terrace is to find and follow the wildlife trail there, but with extreme care because this trail often travels dangerously close to sheer drops.

Hikers who reach the vicinity of lofty Skywalk Arch will find two other large areas of colorful Entrada slickrock to explore on this southern rim of the big mesa.

There is a shorter route to this large arch. Near the upper end of Bartlett Wash, a gigantic rockfall slope allows access to the high bench between the Moab and Slickrock members of the Entrada. From the top of this slope, it is less than two miles to the arch and the slickrock areas in the vicinity.

141

The first person known to reach Skywalk Arch was Los Angeles computer engineer Tom Budlong, on April 17, 1989. He used this shorter route, then explored the Bartlett south wall on downcanyon to the Tusher Canyon saddle and back.

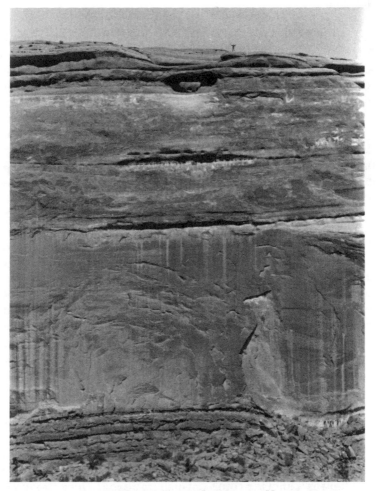

Skywalk Arch and Tom Budlong

SKYWALKING
by Tom Budlong

From the paved road to Dead Horse Point, if you know just where to look, you can see Skywalk Arch. Scurrying along the highway to the famous old horse trap, however, few notice it. Even if you know it's there, and stop at the right place, it's difficult to spot.

Fran Barnes, the author of this book, is a veteran arch hunter and collector, and this span's relative obscurity isn't what bothered him. In fact I think he kind of enjoyed the idea of having something in plain sight but seen by very few.

No, the fact that nobody noticed the arch didn't matter to him. What did matter was that as far as he could tell from the records, no one had ever visited Skywalk Arch. We changed that one nice spring day, and in the process invented "skywalking."

This arch is in the top edge of a 400-foot cliff of what the geologists call Entrada Sandstone. The formation is really three layers -- a relatively thin bottom layer called the Dewey Bridge member; above that the Slickrock member, which is responsible for most of the height; and above that about fifty feet of the whitish Moab member. Having escaped serious geologic convulsions since their deposition, the boundaries between the members here are fairly close to horizontal. The upper Moab member is completely eroded away above the arch, so it is near the top of the Slickrock member of the Entrada.

Why have there never been visitors to Skywalk Arch? Since it is 400-feet straight up from the base of the cliff, you have to approach it from some other direction. And when you try this, from any direction, you realize that the cliff below the arch is just one side of a gigantic, complex plateau, with walls almost straight up all around. (Sorry! Helicopters are unfair!.)

Well, all this wasn't news to Fran -- he had pondered the problem for quite some time while roaming the area, looking for a way up. What he had finally concluded involved a possible route up an immense rubble slope in an alcove on the far side of the plateau, a rubble slope that went up only to the Slickrock-Moab intersection, still 50 feet below the plateau's summit. Well, at least that resolved 350/400ths of the problem of getting up. Once there, of course, it would be an easy walk to the other side, and Skywalk Arch.

Now Fran has a neat trick. He talks people into going places he won't. He's really good at it. That's where I came into the picture. That nice spring day Fran, his wife Terby and I bounced his Land Cruiser around to the back of Big Mesa, as the plateau is called locally, traveling up and down gullies, through sandy washes, over rocks and down sand-dune slopes in the desert floor below the plateau, to the base of that steep rubble slope. With a couple of Terby's roast-beef sandwiches in my day pack, I was soon scrambling up, out of range of Fran's glinting eye.

The climb to the top of the rubble was really easier than it had appeared from below, and that got me almost to the base of the Moab layer, to a slope of bare sandstone near the top of the Slickrock member, but no further. While pondering my next move I noticed several things.

First, I was not alone -- I was being watched from just above by a very nonchalant bighorn ram! Second, the ram was on a shelf formed by the intersection of the top of the Slickrock and bottom of the Moab members. Third, this shelf extended horizontally. In fact, that's how the bighorn got around up there, walking on that intersection shelf. Maybe, I thought, I could do the same until I found a hole in that wall of still higher Moab member that would let me get up to the top.

The shelf width was about 100 feet at its widest. Once I reached it, I started hiking along it, staying close to the inner wall. That was hard work, because that was where all the brush grew, but human instinct demanded that location. Who but a desert sheep wants to walk on the brink of a sheer drop?

As I continued, I found occasional trails that my new friend and his relatives had made. Where the sheep trail veered to the outside, I stuck to the wall. It was still hard work. In time, the hard work got old and tended to melt away the fear of becoming suddenly and fatally detached from the shelf, so I began to follow the sheep trail, even where it went close to the edge. What a wondrous discovery! The sheep had avoided the difficult brush and the many ups and downs that had been giving me such a hard time. They had constructed a well-graded path, just a few inches wide but perfectly walkable -- although right on the rim of the cliff in places! But in no time I was ambling along as nonchalantly as my bighorn guide. Well -- almost.

Although I looked, I never did find a way up through the Moab wall. I just kept going around the plateau, horizontally, staying on the ledge, until the Moab member petered out and allowed me easy access to the plateau top. From there, it was a straight hike of a mile or so to the arch on the other side.

Once there, I climbed up beside the arch, on the edge of its 400-foot cliff, and there were Fran and Terby on the desert floor far below -- they had driven around in their Land Cruiser while I was playing desert sheep.

We let out a few whoops -- the first known personal visit to Skywalk Arch!

Up close I could see that Skywalk was an elegant arch indeed. It was a kind of handle in the edge of the cliff, say 6 feet thick and wide and about 30 feet long. A giant could get a nice grip on the plateau with it. On one side of the arch was that 400-foot cliff. On the other was a huge pothole eroded deeply into the red sandstone. Although the span was easily strong enough and wide enough to permit strolling across, it would take a brave stuntman indeed to do that trick, considering what was on either side. Luke Skywalker, where were you when we needed you?

When I got back down, we speculated on walking that horizontal Slickrock-Moab member intersection and decided we could almost circumnavigate the entire plateau that way. In fact, Fran said he had done exactly that kind of walking for miles, elsewhere on the same immense plateau, and with the same combination of formations elsewhere in the vicinity. Somehow I find that fascinating -- walking continuously, essentially on the rim of a cliff, hundreds of feet off the ground. We decided it was the closest you could get to flying with no machinery involved, so appropriately called it *Skywalking*.

Not a bad day, we decided. Christen an arch and invent a new way of hiking in canyon country. So -- what's for tomorrow, Fran?

Behind Skywalk Arch

Tom Budlong photo

NAME - TUSHER - BARTLETT HIGHLANDS

TYPE - area and route

ROCK - Entrada-Moab member

USE - hiking only

GUIDEBOOK & MAP - *Canyon Country* OFF-ROAD VEHICLE TRAILS - Island Area and matching map

VEHICLE - off-road vehicle

ACCESS

Drive north from Moab on U.S. 191 then west on the Monitor & Merrimac ORV trail, as described in the referenced book and map. At the first junction in about 1/2 mile, take the right hand trail toward Tusher Canyon. Cross the lower Tusher drainage and continue west toward the lower end of Bartlett Wash. Just before this trail drops down to cross the lower Bartlett Wash drainage, turn left on the Bartlett Wash trail, then angle left again within a few yards on a spur trail. Continue on this trail for about 1 mile, to where it branches, with the left trail descending into a valley, and the right trail ascending a steep, eroded grade. Drive or hike up the short right hand trail, to where it ends on a mesa of white slickrock with dark-colored rocks scattered about, just beyond where the mesa is divided by an obvious fault line. The described hiking begins here.

DESCRIPTION

The small mesa where the access trail ends is worth exploring. It also provides the only access route, other than by climbing, to a large, elevated slickrock area that is defined on all sides by sheer cliffs.

The small mesa, which is part Moab member Entrada and part younger deposits, is defined by Bartlett Wash on one side and an unnamed tributary of the complex Tusher Canyon system on the other. It is divided by a major fault line that runs generally east and west. This fault, where the geologic strata have been vertically displaced, is clearly visible on the mesa and in both walls of lower Bartlett Wash, below the mesa. There are several kinds of mineral specimens lying around on the mesa, most from the younger formation but some eroded from the Moab-Entrada.

From the mesa, the first part of the hiking is a route along the summit of the ridge between the canyons that form it. As this ridge begins to ascend, after an initial descent from the small mesa, the slick-rock is set with numerous potholes of various sizes, shapes and depths. During the wetter seasons, many of these potholes contain water. Even during dry seasons, a few still hold some water, and when the combination of water and temperature is right, many of the pools contain populations of tiny cryptobiotic life, including desert shrimp, fairy shrimp, clam shrimp and insect larvae, plus the tadpoles of small amphibians. Since these delicate life forms are fairly rare, and are endangered by human pollution of their only habitats -- the slickrock potholes that occur only in certain desert areas -- it is best to leave undisturbed the unique life cycles of such tiny, isolated biological communities.

Winter hiking, Tusher-Bartlett Highlands

In this area, there are a number of pothole pools that are so extensive and unusually shaped that they are quite beautiful. Hikers who travel on or near the interface of the Entrada Moab-Slickrock interface, on the Bartlett South Rim route described earlier, will note that these pools feed seeping springs at the base of the Entrada-Moab member wall.

Past the main pothole area, the ridge between the canyons widens into an immense area of slickrock, set with a still-higher rubble-sloped butte. Where harder boulders have tumbled down from the younger deposits onto the white, more erodable Entrada-Moab member, the sandstone has eroded selectively from beneath many of the boulders, leaving them perched on tiny pointed pedestals, usually three in number. Such odd balanced rocks are sometimes called "tripod rocks." Tripod rocks perched on slender stone legs as long as two feet and more have been observed. All such delicate erosional oddities should be left undisturbed.

Beyond the first higher butte the ridge narrows, then widens again. A much larger butte occupies most of the next wide section of slickrock, but it is still possible to skirt around the butte's base. Beyond this second butte the main canyon of the Tusher system comes close to joining Bartlett Wash, leaving just a relatively thin sandstone wall between them. It is easy to cross this neck of rock when hiking the Bartlett South Rim route, as described earlier, but climbing aids and skills are required to descend to that level from the top of the Entrada-Moab member being hiked in this description.

Except for the two narrow ridges, hiking in this area is freelance. The best views into the canyon systems below are from near the rims, but the never-ending variety of erosional forms in this area can be found everywhere in the Entrada-Moab member. Rock collectors will find the best hunting near the bases of the two large buttes of younger deposits.

For a sample route, hike along the western rim above Bartlett Wash to the narrows between the two buttes, continue around the northeast side of the second butte for some spectacular views down into the main arm of the Tusher Canyon complex, then return around the rimlands on the east side of the first butte for views down into the branching Tusher tributaries.

There are other areas where it is possible to hike and bike on Entrada-Moab member slickrock, but none offer the unusual erosional features and outstanding viewpoints of this high and isolated area.

Tusher-Bartlett Highlands, aerial photo

149

FISH?

We were hiking with our daughter, who was visiting us from Colorado. It was a bright, windless, warm day in November -- nothing too unusual for canyon country. Just *"another dadgummed beautiful day,"* as we so often told each other.

We had decided to introduce our best and only off-sprat to a place we had found only recently, the elongated peninsula topped by eroded white slickrock that separates two lovely canyons called Bartlett and Tusher. The Moab member Entrada that capped the sloping peninsula had countless potholes in one long, narrow stretch, some of them rather ordinary as potholes go, but most of singular shape and unusual depth.

We had enjoyed the usual lovely autumn that year, with its occasional welcome rain but mostly beautiful, dry, clear weather. The potholes should have plenty of water in them. Some contained water year-around, and harbored isolated communities of water-loving plantlife and tiny animals and insects. Others were transient, showing signs of life only during the warmer months, when the scant summer rain fell. Then, many of the potholes might contain swarming numbers of cryptobiotic species -- fairy, tadpole and clam shrimp -- plus small toad-tadpoles and a number of species of insect larvae.

Tadpole shrimp

The highlight of the pothole stretch of the peninsula was that many of the potholes were quite deep and ornately shaped -- three-dimensional pools worthy of Cleopatra and always at least partially full of clear water. We always enjoyed "discovering" these lovely slickrock ponds and cisterns with each person we took on this hike. We liked to share its unusual beauty and erosional features with people who would appreciate their novelty.

150

We were happily exclaiming about each new discovery -- and those with water were plentiful this time -- when our daughter let out a yip. *"Fish!"*

Fish? -- in a slickrock pool!? Not likely. But even so, I rushed over to see what she had found.

The shallow pool we stood around was perhaps a foot deep, and was swarming with tiny life-forms. A few I recognized -- tadpole shrimp and a scattering of real tadpoles and insect larvae and adults, but the "fish" were new to me. Since I could tell from its lack of permanent water-based vegetation that the pool was transient, not one of the permanent pools in the area, the myriad fish-like creatures less than an inch long simply could not be fish. How could they get there?

Fish are not cryptobiotic. Their eggs cannot stand being totally dehydrated and baked in the scorching-hot sediments in the bottom of a dried-up slickrock pothole, waiting for the right combination of moisture and temperature to re-hydrate them and bring them back to active life. The eggs and larvae of several species of pothole life -- crustaceans and a few insects -- can perform this miracle of adaptation and survival, but no species of fish that I know of.

I watched the tiny creatures for a while, very puzzled. They did, indeed, look like very small fish. They were slender and their bodies were higher than they were wide. They even seemed to swim like fish, wriggling along through the water with their bodies twisting side-to-side. But --

"They can't be fish," I still insisted, while our daughter insisted they were. Finally, I asked her to catch one. She kneeled down beside the pool and quickly scooped up a tiny specimen. We could see its profile as it lay squirming in the bit of water in her palm. From that angle, we could see rows of almost microscopic cilia along it lower edge. It was not a fish -- it was a species of pothole crustacean that we had never seen before. And thriving in a slickrock pothole in mid-November!

The rest of our leisurely hike was highly enjoyable, as we knew it would be, but the highlight of the day was still our transient pool full of myriad desert shrimp -- our "fish" where no fish could be.

151

NAME - TUSHER RIMLANDS

TYPE - area and route

ROCK - Entrada-Slickrock member

USE - hiking and limited biking

GUIDEBOOK & MAP - *Canyon Country* OFF-ROAD VEHICLE TRAILS - Island Area and matching map

VEHICLE - off-road vehicle

ACCESS

Drive north from Moab on U.S. 191 then west on the Monitor & Merrimac ORV trail, as described in the referenced book and map. At the first junction in about 1/2 mile, take the right hand trail toward Tusher Canyon. Cross the lower Tusher drainage and continue west toward the lower end of Bartlett Wash. Just before this trail drops down to cross the lower Bartlett Wash drainage, turn left on the Bartlett Wash trail, then angle left again within a few yards on a spur trail. Continue on this trail for about 1 mile, to where it branches, with the left trail descending into a valley, and the right trail ascending a steep, eroded grade. Drive down the trail to the left to another trail junction at the base of the short grade.

For access to a Tusher Canyon tributary that offers some slick-rock hiking and limited biking, but only after traveling through a stretch of very soft sand, turn right at the base of this short grade. This spur reaches the summit of a short climb in about 1/4 mile, near Tusher Tunnel, one of the few natural tunnels in the region. To reach this feature, hike left for a few hundred feet around the base of the sand-stone ridge where the ORV trail reaches the summit. The tunnel is through the same ridge. Hike or ride down the sandy slope beyond the summit to a large tongue of terraced Entrada-Slickrock in the canyon below.

For access to an excellent slickrock hiking route that is not bikable, drive the trail to the left from the trail junction at the base of the short grade for about 1 mile. Within a few yards of the junction, this trail drops into a shallow wash, then ascends to cross a wide expanse of dune sand. In a little less than 1/2 mile, the trail crosses a shallow wash. In another few yards, the trail reaches a junction on a rocky ridge. Turn right there and continue for another 1/2 mile, to where the trail drops steeply into a sandy wash in the vicinity of several large cottonwood trees. To reach the start of this slickrock hiking route, drive up this wash as far as possible, keeping to the left at a fork near the end of the drivable part of the canyon. Park at the base of a slot-type pouroff just beyond a high sand dune.

Caution: this access route is only for vehicles well equipped for travel in soft sand. There is an alternate access/egress route that is very steep and rocky, but not sandy. When first approaching along the trail to Tusher Canyon, rather than cross it, drive up Tusher Canyon for a little less than 1/2 mile, then turn right on a trail that climbs steeply, then descends even more steeply into the Tusher tributary wash up which it is necessary to drive. This connecting trail between canyons is a little less than 3/4 mile long, but is quite demanding, especially on the return trip.

Tusher Tunnel

DESCRIPTION

From the pouroff where the vehicle access route ends, climb the slickrock slopes to the left toward a high Entrada-Moab member promontory, ascending the terraced slickrock slopes by whatever route is feasible. Near the top of the slickrock, travel left along a terrace through a jumble of fallen rock toward and around an immense, elevated sandstone amphitheater that slopes sharply down into the canyon below the hikable terrace. Just beyond the main curvature of the amphitheater, or anywhere practical within it, climb upward to the top of the sloping slickrock wall, to the flat benchlands at its summit.

From there, ascend the layer of reddish sediments that caps the plateau below the still-higher white promontory, cross these sediments in an easterly direction, then descend to the broad sandstone terrace that marks the top of the Entrada-Slickrock member along the rim of the main branch of Tusher Canyon. The view from along this rim down into the canyon, through the gigantic portal in its opposite wall and on across Courthouse Pasture toward the Determination Towers and the distant La Sal Mountains is outstanding and as colorful as any scene in canyon country.

From one section of this rim, note the small, elevated valley directly below that is formed by a narrow tongue of slickrock. To extend this hiking route somewhat, hike down to this valley by any feasible route, then explore the strange hanging valley and this tongue of slickrock as it climbs to meet the sheer canyon wall.

From the rim, explore the series of descending terraces down into the canyon, and the immense sandstone amphitheater that is below the rim and just downcanyon from the narrow valley, then hike upcanyon on the rim to a large gap in the white Entrada-Moab member wall. Go through this gap, then return downcanyon along the broad, level sandstone rim above the access canyon. Descend into the canyon toward the starting point wherever practical.

For an alternate, more challenging route to the same Tusher Canyon rimlands, from the end of the described vehicle access route climb above the pouroff and hike on up the canyon to its end. From there, climb up the main drainage line in the steep V-shaped slickrock slope. To get around one near-vertical drop in this water-cut drainage, detour to the left up a soil-and-rubble slope before returning to the slickrock. Near the summit of the climb, hike left around the terrace there toward the gap in the higher Entrada-Moab member wall described earlier, then climb the last few feet up onto the broad terrace and on through the gap to the rimlands of the main branch of Tusher Canyon. Descend by the ascent route described earlier.

Whichever approach route is used, allow a full day for this relatively short but demanding hike, so as to have plenty of time to explore and enjoy the outstanding beauty of the sculptured slickrock and the breathtaking canyon-rim panoramas.

155

WHAT NEXT?

We were exploring an area new to us at the time, an area of lovely red-walled canyons, open sand dunes and winding white-sand washes set with occasional bright-green cottonwood trees. We had just visited a long natural tunnel that we later dubbed "Tusher Tunnel," and had just driven our trusty Toyota down a very steep, sandy slope into a wash bottom. I was a bit worried about getting back up that soft slope, but decided to put my trepidations aside for a while and enjoy the spectacular canyon that lay ahead, up the wash. We drove on up Rehsut Canyon.

"Rehsut Canyon"! You can't find it on your map? Little wonder. Rehsut is Tusher spelled backwards. A friend with a quirky sense of humor once applied the unpronounceable name to a splendid, barely-accessible, little-known and unnamed tributary of Tusher. So we both now use the name, at least in writing.

At one point far up the canyon we suddenly reached a barrier that no ordinary wheeled vehicle could surmount, a sandstone pouroff guarded by a high, steep sand dune. We parked and started hiking. We were determined to see the upper end of this deep canyon with its sloping, red lower walls and still higher setback-walls of white sandstone -- Entrada slickrock and Moab members.

At the head of the canyon, the going got tough. The sandy wash and rocky rubble ended, but still ahead of us was an inviting slope of reddish slickrock, vertically notched by millennia of transient rain runoff. I felt lured up that V-shaped slope, like mythical sailors onto hazardous shoreline rocks. Up I went, with my wife close behind, probably shaking her head in wonder. She knows I don't like steep places -- and this slope was steep!

Up we went, higher and higher, then laterally now and then, seeking ways around stretches that were too steep for even the stickiest of boot-soles. Then on upward. Once, we had to leave the slickrock entirely because of an overhanging ledge that crossed the entire steep drainage. We used an even steeper slope of fallen rubble and accumulated soils held in place by trees and brush to get above the ledge, then returned to the slickrock.

Finally, we reached the top of the sloping wall -- almost. There was still one final undercut ledge to surmount. We had to travel horizontally for a hundred feet or more before finding a place where a fallen boulder allowed us to help each other on up.

Once on the broad terrace that marked the usual interface between the two Entrada members, we hiked on through the enormous portal there, a gap in the higher Moab member between Tusher and Rehsut canyons, and then walked downcanyon on the broad slickrock interface on the Tusher side.

Had anyone ever before visited this lofty, isolated world of colorful slickrock and bright sky? There was certainly no evidence of it if they had. The whole area, as far as we could see, showed no sign that mankind even existed -- if you didn't squint into the sun and spot a few distant wheel tracks in the sandy bottom of Tusher Canyon. A world primeval, untouched by man!

But what was this just ahead? Something too geometric in shape broke the natural irregularity of the dominating erosion patterns and occasional harder pebbles that were scattered across the white sandstone terrace on which we were strolling.

I picked it up, a small object made of metal. Certainly, no wheeled vehicle had ever been here. Besides, this was no auto part. I studied it closely. A very hard alloy, forged then machined to close tolerances, and shaped into a curving double-flange. My long-dorment aerospace engineering past woke up and said -- *"airplane part."* Airplane part? Here?

After further thought, we stuck to that hunch. When the probable doesn't work, you're stuck with the improbable. The area we were in does suffer a certain amount of air traffic overhead, from the nearby Grand County airport. Some time in the past, for some reason, a plane had lost a part while overflying the high sandstone ridge that separates Tusher and Rehsut canyons. We hoped the loss didn't mess up the plane's landing.

What next!?

NAME - T U S H E R - M I L L P E N I N S U L A

TYPE - area and route

ROCK - Entrada-Slickrock member

USE - hiking and biking

GUIDEBOOK & MAP - *Canyon Country* **OFF-ROAD VEHICLE TRAILS - Island Area** and matching map

VEHICLE - off-road vehicle

ACCESS

Drive north from Moab on U.S. 191 then west on the Monitor & Merrimac ORV trail, as described in the referenced book and map. At the first junction in about 1/2 mile, take the right hand trail toward Tusher Canyon. Where this trail enters the shallow wash of lower Tusher Canyon, drive up the wash and into the lower canyon. Park anywhere beyond the spring-wet narrows, in the vicinity of an abandoned drill site that is on a terrace above and to the left of the wash bottom. A very eroded ORV trail climbs up toward the drill site and provides easy access to the broad slickrock terrace that marks the beginning of the described hiking route.

158

DESCRIPTION

From the narrows of lower Tusher Canyon it is possible to hike both the west and east walls of this magnificent canyon. The convoluted, elongated area of slickrock that forms the west side of Tusher Canyon is less spectacular at first, but eventually enters the immense and pictur-esque amphitheater seen from above, as noted earlier in the Tusher Rimlands description. This approach to the Tusher Rimlands provides easier access, but misses the challenge and beauty of ascending from the described Tusher tributary canyon.

The sloping, terraced eastern wall of Tusher Canyon ascends to end at a distant point where the drainages of Tusher and Mill canyon, the next canyon to the east, have broken through the wall that separates them, leaving a wide gap. All of the intricately eroded canyons, bowls and elevated peninsulas of this point are worth exploring, and the views from there of Tusher Canyon, Courthouse Pasture, the Monitor and Merrimac buttes, and the distant La Sal Mountains are outstanding.

To reach the lofty point and its vertical maze of red slickrock, hike or bike up any convenient sandstone ledge or terrace, climbing up ledges to higher levels as necessary. Bikers will find it necessary to lift and carry their bikes occasionally along this route, but will encounter few limits to exploring at the summit.

At the summit of the point, several hanging slickrock canyons invite exploration. The two longest are carved from solid rock and end by plunging abruptly into the deep narrows of Mill Canyon. There are pools of water in both canyons during the wetter months.

The ultimate end of the point is on a high, slender promontory dominated by weather-rounded red and gray sandstone.

From this point, the view in all directions is breathtaking. Directly below is the immense gap in the high rock wall that separates Tusher and Mill canyons. Magnificent Tusher Canyon lies to the west, and the narrows of Mill Canyon are visible to the north. To the east and south, the broad dune-and-slickrock expanse of Courthouse Pasture is set with several massive red and white sandstone buttes and the dark red Determination Towers. The Monitor & Merrimac buttes define the sloping lowlands in the near-distance, and the La Sal Mountains mark the distant horizon.

Return to the canyon floor from the point by the same route, or by an alternate route on top of the white Entrada-Moab member sandstone that caps the sloping peninsula formed by Tusher and Mill canyons. The best alternate route closely parallels the Tusher Canyon rim. This return route is not practical for bikers, and requires hiking back up the canyon for a short distance to the parked vehicle.

NAME - D U M A P O I N T

TYPE - area

ROCK - Entrada-Slickrock member

USE - hiking and limited biking

GUIDEBOOK & MAP - *Canyon Country* **OFF-ROAD VEHICLE TRAILS - Island Area** and matching map

VEHICLE - off-road vehicle or high-clearance highway vehicle

ACCESS

Drive north from Moab on U.S. 191, then west on the Blue Hills Road just south of the airport, as described in the referenced book and map. After about 13 miles, turn southwest on the Duma Point Road. After another 5-1/2 miles, the enormous mass of salmon-hued slickrock to the north is Duma Point. Park and hike.

For hiking access to the Duma Point slickrock from the southwest, drive past the point, then turn right on the Red Wash ORV trail. Vehicles without off-road capabilities should exercise caution on this trail.

DESCRIPTION

Duma Point offers more than a square mile of colorful Entrada-Slickrock domes, canyons, terraces and amphitheaters to explore. Some of the lower slopes and terraces can be traveled by mountain bikes, but extensive exploration of this area's eroded complexity requires hiking, and some careful free-climbing to attain its higher levels.

In some of the lower valleys and small canyons in the area, large black intrusions add contrast to the colorful scene. These curious anomalies probably acquired their color from a manganese mineral. How they formed is a geologic mystery, but they may represent places where mineral-laden water seeped upward through an overburden of dune sand.

Views from this slickrock area toward the west include the bright-hued drainage of Red Wash, the Green River gorge in the distance, and still more hikable Entrada-Slickrock masses beyond the river. For details about how to reach and explore the slickrock beyond the river, refer to **THE LABYRINTH RIMS** guide book.

NAME - BRINKS - LUNAR CANYONS

TYPE - area

ROCK - Entrada-Slickrock and Entrada-Moab members

USE - hiking and biking

GUIDEBOOK & MAP - *Canyon Country* OFF-ROAD VEHICLE TRAILS - Island Area and matching map

VEHICLE - off-road vehicle

ACCESS

Drive north from Moab on U.S. 191, west on the Blue Hills Road then south on the Hidden Canyon Rim ORV trail, as described in the referenced book and map. After the trail has gone about 1/4 mile beyond Brink Spring, Brinks Canyon appears on the left.

Beyond this narrow canyon, watch for a spur trail that ascends a low ridge of sediments on the right, then descends into a broad slickrock area. This is Lunar Canyon.

Lunar Canyon

164

DESCRIPTION

The broad Entrada-Moab member rimlands of Brinks Canyon offer a large expanse of hikable, bikable slickrock, with views down into this long, narrow gorge. Hikers can explore the enchanting depths of Brinks Canyon by walking its sloping Entrada-Slickrock walls, or by finding routes up the canyon at other levels. To get into the canyon, hike down the steep rubble slope near the canyon's lower end, just downcanyon of where it is cut by a major geologic fault line.

There is a small cave beneath the southern Entrada-Moab rim of this canyon, and an immense alcove at its upper end, with seeping springs and hanging gardens of water-loving vegetation. The main drainage of the canyon above the alcove makes an interesting hiking route, and in places the surrounding slickrock provides a playground for gymnastic bikers.

Lunar Valley lies parallel to Brinks Canyon to the northwest. It offers an irregular square mile of eroded slickrock completely enclosed by higher ridges of broken sandstone and sediments. The white slickrock valley is cut by a complex system of drainage lines that are little bar to hiking, but that make direct progress across the valley a challenge to bikers.

Exploring this small but enchanting "lunar landscape" is preferable during the cooler months, but its intricacies offer both hikers and bikers some interesting challenges. The nearby rimlands of Hidden Canyon, at the end of the main access trail, are also worth exploring while in this area, for both hikers and bikers.

Lower Brinks Canyon

Upper Brinks Canyon

FLASH-FLOOD!

It was a bright, sunny day in late January -- too cold for extensive hiking, but fine for some exploring in enclosed off-road vehicles, with occasional short hikes. Two families of us were doing just that, anxious to work off some of the seasonal *blahs* we had accumulated during an especially cold winter.

After driving up the deeply shadowed and frozen wonderland of lower Mill Canyon, we turned out onto the northern part of Courthouse Pasture, the sunlit slickrock area to the south of Mill-Courthouse Mesa, then parked for a short exploratory hike before lunch.

The broad expanse of white Navajo slickrock was almost blindingly bright. Each of the thousands of shallow potholes on the hundreds of acres of sandstone contained it own large disc of solid ice, and crusty snow lay in thick patches everywhere else. The tops of the red-walled cliffs that loomed above us showed few traces of snow, but there was doubtless plenty on the levels back from the rims. This became all-too evident quite soon.

After we all had grown chilled from hiking around in this snow-and-ice-and-slickrock wonderland, we sought the protection of our vehicles and the comfort of the hot drinks in our lunches. The winter sun quickly warmed the vehicles like greenhouses.

As we ate, something wondrous began to happen. A warm south wind came up -- an early breath of spring. We marveled at the sudden change of temperature. Then the crusty remnants of snow, and the ice in the nearby potholes, began to melt. Icy water started trickling from one pothole to the next, then joined the hundreds of similar trickles from nearby potholes. These in turn joined still larger brooklets of ice-melt, forming flowing streams that quickly joined again to form still larger streams.

As we marveled at this miraculous transformation of quiet, motionless winter solitude into myriad gurgling creeks flowing rapidly and noisily across a huge expanse of slickrock, someone broke the spell and we all glanced up at the distant salmon-colored cliffline of Entrada-slickrock sandstone. There we saw another unbelievable scene -- two slender, blood-hued waterfalls plunging hundreds of feet down into the canyon, from narrow clefts in the lofty cliff-top! Clouds of brownish mist rose from where they met the rocks far below.

As I watched the eerie sight of waterfalls originating from what appeared to be the highest point in sight, I made myself a promise to someday see where those colorful ribbons of snow-melt were coming from, and explore the canyons that collected and channeled the water to its spectacular plunge downward.

We eventually did find a way up into that colorful, alluring sandstone wonderland. It became one of our favorite slickrock hiking goals -- the Tusher-Mill Peninsula.

But at the time, another matter soon occupied our attention. If we stayed much longer where we were on that broad expanse of slickrock with its melting pothole ice, we might be in trouble. To get there, we had crossed an inconspicuous drainage line that was not very deep, but it soon occurred to me that all that snow-melt had to go somewhere, and its nearest route toward lower terrain was down the wash we had crossed!

By the time we drove back to the wash it was too late. A veritable torrent of water was rushing down the rocky draw. We were not going back by that route, at least for several hours. Fortunately, I knew of another way to leave the broad expanse of slickrock, so I drove south, past the towering mass of another sandstone butte, then across a series of sandstone outcrops to a spur trail that could be used to leave the Courthouse Pasture area.

Before leaving, however, we drove around to the far side of the flooding canyon and photographed its racing waters. It was a fascinating sight, now that we had escaped its threat. A late-winter flash-flood, under bright blue skies!

NAME - MILL - COURTHOUSE DRAINAGE

TYPE - area

ROCK - Navajo Sandstone

USE - hiking and biking

GUIDEBOOK & MAP - *Canyon Country* OFF-ROAD VEHICLE TRAILS - Island Area and matching map

VEHICLE - off-road vehicle or high-clearance highway vehicle, depending on access point used

ACCESS

Drive north from Moab on U.S. 191, then west on the Monitor & Merrimac ORV trail as described in the referenced book and map. At the first junction in about 1/2 mile, turn left. In another 1/2 mile, the righthand trail enters the slickrock area via a short spur from the ORV trail that goes up Mill Canyon. The spur goes left just beyond the upper end of the canyon narrows. This approach requires an off-road vehicle.

The lefthand trail at the second junction enters the slickrock area via Courthouse Canyon. It can be traveled to the area by high-clearance highway vehicles when the trail is in good condition, but drivers of such vehicles should be very cautious.

Upper Courthouse drainage

To enter the upper narrows of Courthouse Canyon, drive a few yards south from the trail junction, then angle right onto another spur trail in the bottom of a drainage line that is often wet from springs higher in the drainage. This spur goes past the historic, partly restored "Halfway Stage Station," an overnight stopping place for early travelers between Moab and settlements to the north, then continues into the canyon narrows where it shortly drops down onto the hikable, bikable slickrock area.

It is also possible to reach the described slickrock area from other segments of the Monitor & Merrimac ORV trail, by watching for unmapped spur trails that approach this large area of white Navajo Sandstone.

Spring-fed grottoes, Upper Courthouse drainage

171

DESCRIPTION

This area is a broad expanse of sloping Navajo Sandstone set with soaring buttes and ridges of colorful Entrada-Slickrock and cut by intricate canyons, many of them with linear pools of water in deep crevices. One of the big sandstone buttes had long, slender Courthouse Arch high in its western flank. The lovely arch collapsed in the winter of 1988-1989.

The upper drainages of both Mill and Courthouse canyons have cut deeply into the slickrock, making complex slots and grottoes, some of which contain permanent pools of water.

This area provides a broad expanse of somewhat tilted slickrock that offers both hikers and bikers the opportunity for extensive routeless freelance exploring, in a spectacular setting of immense, colorful Entrada sandstone buttes and walls. Bikers will find this area to be fairly easy to explore, yet fascinating in its variety of erosional forms.

173

NAME - MILL - COURTHOUSE MESA

TYPE - area

ROCK - Entrada-Moab and Entrada-slickrock members

USE - hiking only

GUIDEBOOK & MAP - *Canyon Country* OFF-ROAD VEHICLE TRAILS - Island Area and matching map

VEHICLE - high-clearance highway vehicle

ACCESS

Drive north from Moab on U.S. 191, then west on the Monitor & Merrimac ORV trail as described in the referenced book and map. In 1/2 mile, turn left at a trail junction, then left again in another 1/2 mile. Within a few yards, as this trail crosses a drainage line, angle right onto a spur trail. Travel this for about 1/4 mile, then park at the historic "Halfway Stage Station," or continue past this for another 1/4 mile to a small pull-out just before the trail descends steeply. The hike begins here.

Courthouse Rock, viewed from Mill-Courthouse Mesa

DESCRIPTION

Mill-Courthouse Mesa is a high, sheer-walled sandstone mesa with a sloping, isolated summit more than a square mile in size that overlooks Mill and Courthouse canyons, their slickrock upper drainages, Courthouse Pasture with its tall towers and isolated buttes, and the gigantic Monitor & Merrimac buttes. The mesa provides a breathtaking 360-degree panorama from its highest reaches.

Getting up onto the mesa is the first problem, and one of the challenges of exploring this elevated slickrock area. From the ORV trail pull-out that is 1/4 mile beyond the historic wagon station, the route is fairly easy to find. Climb the rocky crest to the right, or west, of the trail, then cross the broad valley beyond the crest to its far ridgeline.

Hike left, or south, along this ridge toward a large prominence in the top of the cliff being approached. This jutting monolith of white sandstone is about 100 yards right of the spires that mark the corner of the Courthouse cliffline, and is directly above a sloping alcove of red sandstone. Hike into this alcove by any feasible route, then climb above it to the right. Continue right, climbing steeply. The obvious route ends in a narrow cleft behind a jutting slab of sandstone, where the limbs of a sturdy pinion tree offer the only way on up. Note the small rock cairn on the rim at this point. It marks the way back down.

Almost up!

175

Once on top of the mesa, freelance exploring is in order. One way to sample this large, isolated expanse of slickrock is to hike around its perimeter. The nearest rim to the ascent point is that of Courthouse Canyon, to the left, or east, but hiking around the mesa in either direction is rewarding. Both Courthouse and Mill canyons are hundreds of feet below the mesa-top, and along the south-facing rim the view to the south across Courthouse Pasture toward the Monitor & Merrimac is breathtaking. To the west, the ornate rimlands of Mill-Tusher Point loom above the gigantic sandstone portal between these two canyons.

The top of Mill-Courthouse Mesa is much like other areas of Entrada-Moab member slickrock. Its upper surface is cut by jointing and erosion into giant "biscuits" of rock, with deep crevices and slots between them. There are numerous ornate potholes in the more level surfaces. Almost always some of them are water-filled from recent rain or melting snow. During the warmer months, some of these potholes may host swarms of ephemeral life forms, such as tadpoles, tiny pothole shrimp and various stages of desert insect life.

Along the edges of the mesa, accelerated erosion has carved tiny canyons, grottoes and alcoves into the rock, many of them cut deeply into the underlying salmon-hued Entrada-Slickrock sandstone. On the southern edge of the mesa, the white Moab member Entrada has eroded completely away, leaving a large, sloping area of rounded, weathered salmon-hued Slickrock member. There is a large pothole-lake in this area that generally contains water, but which is not accessible without climbing aids.

Altogether, the lofty, isolated world of Mill-Courthouse Mesa is well worth the extra effort it takes to visit it.

Slickenslides Arch in Courthouse Rock

Views from the south end of Mill-Courthouse Mesa

NAME - TENMILE CANYON RIMS

TYPE - areas

ROCK - Navajo Sandstone

USE - hiking and limited biking

GUIDEBOOKS& MAP - *Canyon Country* OFF-ROAD VEHICLE TRAILS - **Island Area** and matching map, and **THE LABYRINTH RIMS** by Jack Bickers

VEHICLE - off-road vehicle

ACCESS

Drive north from Moab on U.S. 191, west on Blue Hills Road, then southwest on Duma Point Road as described in the referenced books and map. Follow the directions in **THE LABYRINTH RIMS** book for various access points to the rimlands of long Tenmile Canyon and its remote confluence with the Labyrinth Canyon stretch of the Green River.

Tenmile Canyon Rims -- Jack Bickers photo

DESCRIPTION

This intermittent but immense expanse of Navajo Sandstone slickrock is too extensive to describe in detail. The entire rimlands of this spectacular canyon complex have been carved by eons of erosion from desert-aeolian Navajo Sandstone. This has left a highly complex maze cut deeply into white sandstone, a maze consisting of the labyrinthine canyon itself, plus the myriad complications created by its numerous tributaries.

Above these deep, twisting gorges, the rimlands are a maze of slickrock domes, fins, grottoes, alcoves, seeping springs, caves, tall towers and grotesque monoliths, in places for a mile or more back from the rim of the main canyon. Toward the lower end of Tenmile Canyon, its rimlands are almost solid, unbroken slickrock ledges, terraces, domes and jutting sandstone peninsulas, with breathtaking views into the main and tributary canyons from hundreds of spectacular rim viewpoints.

As described in **THE LABYRINTH RIMS** book, there are ways for hikers, and even off-road vehicles, to cross Tenmile Canyon from one rim to the other. This permits hikers and bikers who approach the canyon via these access routes to explore areas along both rims from one access, and also provides the chance to camp overnight in the canyon in one of its shady cottonwood groves.

The only practical way to explore this immense slickrock area is to choose one of the many access points described in the two referenced books, then start freelance hiking from wherever the terrain looks attractive. While bikers will find fewer places practical for their form of exploring, there are still enough places in this area of canyon country to keep any biker busy for days. Altogether, many days, or even weeks, could be spent exploring the complexities of the Tenmile Canyon Rims.

Since there are relatively few places in this area to escape from the hot desert sun during the warmer months, this area is best explored during the cooler months, from February through May, and from September through November. If access is practical, even some winters are mild enough to permit exploring this remote sandstone wilderness area.

"The Mercats" rock formation -- Jack Bickers photo

Tenmile Canyon Rims -- Jack Bickers photo

NAME - LOWER LITTLE CANYON

TYPE - route

ROCK - Kayenta Sandstone

USE - hiking only

GUIDEBOOK & MAP - *Canyon Country* OFF-ROAD VEHICLE TRAILS - Island Area and matching map

VEHICLE - off-road vehicle

ACCESS

Drive north from Moab on U.S. 191, then south on the Gemini Bridges ORV trail as described in the referenced book and map. Stay on the trail as it climbs above the paved highway, descends into and down the main branch of Little Canyon, then angles left at the base of a steep grade that climbs out of the canyon. Stay on the trail down the canyon drainage as far as practical for vehicles then park where the slickrock hiking begins.

DESCRIPTION

The lower Little Canyon drainage cuts down through the ledgy rock of the Kayenta Formation for several miles, before plunging over impassible Wingate cliffs. It is not practical to hike the entire meandering route on solid slickrock. Some washbottom hiking on sand and gravel is necessary, but the water-carved rock stretches at intervals along the main drainage are well worth a little slogging through the occasional stretches of sand that are typical of Kayenta hiking.

Wherever the water has cut through Kayenta sandstone, there are lovely, complex grottoes and labyrinths, many with permanent pools of water. In places it is possible to hike the slickrock terraces above the drainage line, with a little agility where gaps in the rock appear. In a few places such detours are necessary in order to bypass pools, or pouroffs too steep or narrow for passage. Numerous gnarled cottonwood trees along the canyon bottom offer shade during warmer days, and many short sidecanyons and broad slickrock terraces invite exploring by the more adventurous hikers.

Eventually, the main drainage line reaches a wide, sheer pouroff that seems to defy further progress, but a hike to the right along slickrock ledges and down a steep, rocky slope permits the hike to continue on down another shallow canyon to the distant inner gorge of the Colorado River, and more miles of exploratory slickrock hiking.

NAME - CULVERT CANYON

TYPE - area and route

ROCK - Kayenta Sandstone

USE - hiking only

GUIDEBOOK & MAP - any highway map of southeastern Utah

VEHICLE - highway vehicle

ACCESS

Drive downriver from U.S. 191 on Utah 279, as shown on any map of southeastern Utah, to Gold Bar Bend, about 10-1/2 miles from where the state highway leaves U.S. 191. Park where a large metal culvert goes under the railroad embankment just above road-level.

Culvert Canyon grotto

184

DESCRIPTION

The Culvert Canyon drainage encompasses a large area of Kayenta sandstone on one tilted monocline of the Moab Valley anticline. Because of its slope, it is possible to hike up this steep canyon yet still remain entirely within the Kayenta Formation. The main drainage line of the canyon makes an excellent hiking route that provides the best of Kayenta slickrock hiking.

The hiking route begins by going through the large culvert beneath the railroad tracks. Within a few hundred feet, it is necessary to climb out to the right, then back down again, in order to bypass a large permanent pool below a pouroff. For much of the next mile, the hiking in the drainage line is on solid slickrock, with an occasional grotto or patch of huge boulders to get around, and pools here and there during the wetter months.

Then the canyon forks three ways. The right fork and the one straight ahead soon end in large boulder patches and slopes at the bases of soaring cliffs of Navajo Sandstone. The left fork shortly ends in a large alcove, but that can be bypassed by climbing ledges before entering this short spur canyon, then dropping back down into the drainage above the pouroff. The eroded slickrock grotto just above the pouroff is interesting.

Another few hundred yards up the drainage there is another pouroff and a spring-seep alcove. This one has a permanent pool at its base, and generally has at least some water dripping into it from above. Note this pouroff and hike back to it from above. The drainage back from its lip is a lovely, green Eden.

To get around the pouroff, hike up the broad ledges on the right side of the canyon, a few yards back from the alcove. Watch below for the deeply-cut grotto carved into solid rock back from the pouroff, and get back down into the main drainage at the first opportunity, where a series of narrow rock ledges permit descent to the slickrock canyon floor. There, walk back down the drainage on the far side, into the echoing, undercut grotto just above the last pouroff, where other permanent pools play host to water-loving vegetation in an idyllic setting.

Up the main drainage from the descent point, watch for a small natural bridge, and from the extreme right side of the drainage in the vicinity of the bridge, watch the highest slickrock mass above the west wall of the canyon for the immense opening of Jeep Arch. It is possible to hike on up and out of Culvert Canyon to this picturesque natural rock opening, after exploring the rest of the wide expanse of Kayenta slickrock in its upper drainage.

For energetic hikers, it is even possible to continue up the monocline slope to the distant Gold Bar Rim, high above the northern end of Moab Valley and the developed entryway to Arches National Park, with outstanding panoramic views in all directions.

While in this vicinity, adventurous hikers might like to look for Barrette Arch, a 123-foot natural span that was first reported in 1989, despite its proximity to well-traveled ORV trails. The arch is visible from the opening of Jeep Arch, about 1/2 mile away and just east of north, and is about 1/3 mile down from the Gold Bar Rim in the head of one upper tributary of Gold Bar Canyon. There are two other smaller natural spans on down the same drainage.

Jeep Arch

SKYLAND

Courthouse Pasture is an immense, sloping meadowland of sand, sage, blackbrush, red towers and white slickrock. It begins at the lofty rimlands of Upper Sevenmile Canyon and the rims that loom even higher above the main highway through canyon country. It then slopes gently toward the north. Most of the water that falls on this gigantic sand-and-slickrock area drains northward through two canyons that have carved deeply between soaring red sandstone buttes capped with white, plus still-higher layers of younger rubble and sediments.

One canyon is called Mill, the other Courthouse. Between these is a butte, a separate remainder of the lofty highlands that still dominate Courthouse Pasture on its western flank. We call this towering, isolated butte Mill-Courthouse Mesa.

For years, we had gazed up at this sky-island, this sheer-walled, slope-topped square mile of slickrock-in-the-heavens, and had looked for a way up onto its top, a way that could be hiked, not climbed, but to no avail. We had long since given up on its three sheer sides, and had spent considerable time studying its lower, more broken northern wall with binoculars, still without finding a feasible route to the top.

That northern wall was tempting, luring. It was defined by a gigantic fault line that ran roughly east and west. The land to the south of the fault had long ago been displaced upward in some monstrous geologic spasm, creating a broken, irregular cliffline when exposed by the last ten megayears of erosion. Still, most of the cliff was just too steep and hazardous for anyone to ascend without climbing aids and skills.

We had given up on ever attaining the summit of Mill-Courthouse Mesa, and had almost forgotten it existed, when a friend happened to mention finding a way up onto a high butte. After a bit of discussion, our friend's butte turned out to be our mesa, so a few days later we set out with our new clues, hoping finally to reach our long-abandoned goal -- the summit of our unattainable skyland.

Our instructions were kind of vague, but one unforgettable clue stuck in our minds. The last little climb at the upper ridge was made possible by a handy pinyon tree. Aha!

So, after driving as close to the cliff as practical, I searched the northern cliff-line for a tree that might be our ladder to the top, using powerful, wide-angle binoculars. There were quite a few trees near the summit of that long rim, but few that might be approached safely from below. Of these, one looked especially promising, so we set off in separate directions up the steep, rubbly slope below it.

My wife took the shortest route, which I preferred to avoid because it soon traveled a narrow ledge above a deadly drop. Instead I started climbing a steep slope that was part rubble, part severely weathered slickrock. She got to the tree first, because my route became quite hazardous toward the top, and even more hazardous to descend for another start. So I persisted.

I caught up with her on a narrow but relatively safe ledge, high above the broken terrain to the north, and just below the final rock-notch that granted passage upward -- with the help of a large, sturdy pinyon tree. After a minute of monkey-work up the tree, and a few more feet of slickrock scrambling, we stood on the lofty rim, triumphant at long last!

There's nothing quite so satisfying as scratching a long-time itch!

After catching our breath, we headed for the nearest higher rim, that of Courthouse Canyon. There, we walked for a few hundred feet along the broken and eroded rim and took a few hasty pictures, before starting back down. We had headed that day for another place, needing some pictures there for a book that was close to being ready to send to the printer. But having finally conquered our nemesis, with the help of a dear friend, we promised ourselves we would return soon and thoroughly explore this square mile of mysterious, isolated slickrock.

That promise was not kept. Shortly thereafter, an early-winter snow fell and didn't melt, and even a little snow on the north cliff-face that had to be climbed was enough to make the ascent hazardous for anyone but skilled ice-climbers, so we had to wait until the following spring to explore further.

But when we did, we found that our lofty "skyland" was an even more fascinating place than we could have hoped. The two uppermost Entrada Sandstone members make excellent slickrock hiking almost anywhere, but the top of this mesa was exceptional in its beauty and variety.

It was well worth the years of frustration and waiting.

NAME - GOLD BAR CANYON

TYPE - area and route

ROCK - Kayenta and Wingate sandstones

USE - hiking only

GUIDEBOOK & MAP - any highway map of southeastern Utah

VEHICLE - highway vehicle

ACCESS

Drive downriver from U.S. 191 on Utah 279, as shown on any map of southeastern Utah, to Gold Bar Bend, about 10-1/2 miles from where this highway leaves U.S. 191. Either park by the road, or drive up the dirt road near the boat-launch ramp toward the elevated railroad tracks and park there. This road is too eroded for normal highway vehicles to travel all the way up.

DESCRIPTION

Gold Bar Canyon is roughly parallel to Culvert Canyon and much like it in that it is a sloping drainage that travels almost entirely through Kayenta slickrock, with Navajo Sandstone walls looming high above its lower end. Gold Bar Canyon, however, is more difficult to hike because of a series of pouroffs that require considerable climbing up and down rock ledges to bypass.

At the railroad tracks, hike left, or west, along the tracks, as they cross lower Culvert Canyon. On the left side of this canyon, hike up the eroded remnant of an old jeep trail that climbs steeply to a fence segment, then around the fence and on up the old trail until it levels off somewhat.

Continue up the slope toward the lofty point of cliff that separates Culvert Canyon and the next canyon downriver, which is Gold Bar Canyon. Skirt left around the cliff base toward some immense boulders, then start descending onto the upper rim of Gold Bar Canyon just beyond the boulders.

The first mile or so of Gold Bar Canyon is cut into Wingate Sandstone and is divided by three impassable pouroffs. The canyon between the railroad fill and the first pouroff is brushy and cannot be reached from the rim, but is not worth hiking. It is possible to get into the stretch between the first and second pouroffs by at least two routes down. There is a nice stretch of water-sculpted slickrock, some trees and several delightful pools of water in this stretch of canyon.

It is easier to get down into the drainage between the second and third pouroffs. This stretch has more pools, trees and slickrock, plus a delightful little natural bridge. Beside the bridge, a natural tunnel penetrates perhaps 50 feet under the rock. The tunnel is floored by a permanent, fairly deep pool of clear, cold water. In mid-day, the water is lit by shafts of sunlight that slip through crevices in the tunnel ceiling.

Above the third pouroff, the going is easier for some distance, with stretches of slickrock alternating with open, sandy wash and trees, and lower rock walls. Eventually, about 1-1/2 miles from the canyon mouth, the drainage intersects one spur of the Gold Bar Rim ORV trail. This trail can be used as a pick-up or drop-off point, or the hike can continue on up the drainage beyond the vehicle trail to lofty and spectacular Gold Bar Rim.

It is possible, but with some difficulty, to continue on up the drainage to where it again cuts deeply into the steeply-sloping Wingate, carving a complex of branching canyons deep within this colorful rock. Exploring these tilted, V-bottomed canyons is a challenging and unique experience.

Hikers should note that the steep upper stretches of Gold Bar Canyon are more difficult to hike because of narrows, ledges and other obstacles to direct progress. A certain amount of backtracking and scrambling up ledges is required, but this is part of the challenge of slick-rock exploring.

As noted in the Culvert Canyon description, there are three natural spans in one of the uppermost tributaries of Gold Bar Canyon, one of them quite large. Reaching them by hiking up the Gold Bar drainage is difficult but possible, although it requires short detours out of the drainage to bypass pouroffs.

Belt-Buckle Arch

Barrette Arch,

upper

Gold Bar Canyon

NAME - POISON SPIDER - GOLD BAR RIMS

TYPE - area

ROCK - Navajo and Kayenta sandstones

USE - hiking and biking

GUIDEBOOK & MAP - *Canyon Country* OFF-ROAD VEHICLE TRAILS - Island Area and matching map

VEHICLE - off-road vehicle

ACCESS

For access to the Gold Bar Rim end of this immense slickrock area, drive north from Moab on U.S. 191, then south on the Gemini Bridges ORV trail, as described in the referenced book and map. From the Little Canyon trail junction, drive up the main Gold Bar Rim ORV trail to wherever the slickrock hiking looks appealing.

For access to the Poison Spider Mesa end of this immense slickrock area, drive down the Colorado River gorge on Utah 279, then up the Poison Spider Mesa ORV trail to wherever the slickrock hiking looks appealing. There are several good areas available from various points on this trail.

Behind the Rocks, from Poison Spider Mesa

194

DESCRIPTION

Although this area has two names on maps, it is essentially one long ridge that is the summit of one monocline of the Moab Valley anticline. Its entire surface is steeply sloped. This has allowed erosion to cut deeply into the ridge many places, creating a number of strangely-shaped, red-walled canyons, and dividing the long ridge into its two major segments.

The Poison Spider Mesa end of the ridge is largely Navajo Sandstone, while the Gold Bar Rim end is largely Kayenta, with little Navajo remaining. This provides both scenic and hiking variety. The panorama from any part of the highest rim is outstanding. The view to the west is dominated by the intricate, deeply-cut meanders of the Colorado River gorge. Moab Valley sprawls below, and the exotic rock shapes of Arches National Park and the lofty La Sal Mountains cover the entire eastern horizon.

From the Gold Bar Rim approach, the hikable slickrock begins within a mile of where the ORV trail climbs out of Little Canyon and continues to the high rim, offering hikers several days of excellent slickrock exploring, either by backpack or by day-hikes from a vehicle basecamp. Among the highlights to seek in this area are Jeep Arch and Barrette Arch, as noted in the Culvert Canyon description, and a rim view down into the canyon where the tall, slender spire of The Bride stands. The entire area is a veritable maze of deep gorges, smaller canyons, picturesque ledges and mysterious crevices, all cut into Kayenta sandstone or the more colorful Wingate just below.

The Bride

From the Poison Spider Mesa approach, there are at least four somewhat separate slickrock areas worth exploring, two of them quite large.

The first occurs just a few yards beyond where the ORV access trail levels off after climbing a series of switchbacks then crossing a small drainage that is sometimes wet from spring-seepage. The broad canyon to the right of the trail has two highlights. Graceful Longbow Arch stands out from the wall of a small tributary gorge in the right side of the canyon at its upper end, and it is possible to hike up the steep slickrock slopes on the right, near the center of the canyon, to a high ridge that overlooks the Colorado River gorge and the spectacular sandstone fins of Behind-the-Rocks. This side route offers a fairly large area of eroded slickrock well worth exploring.

Longbow Arch

The second and third hiking areas occur about 2 miles from where the ORV access trail leaves Utah 279, just before the trail enters a narrow canyon. The two areas are separated for practical purposes by the canyon the vehicle trail enters. To explore the one to the right, hike across a small valley then ascend the slickrock dome to the right at its upper end. Beyond the valley, by angling to the left, it is possible to climb to the summits of several giant ridges of Navajo slickrock, with spectacular panoramas to the south and west across still more wildly eroded sandstone domes and fins.

The hiking route to the left of the ORV trail begins by ascending through the eroded cleft of an elevated drainage, then climbing to higher levels. From there on the hiking is freestyle, with a maze of slickrock domes, terraces, canyons and giant grottoes worth exploring.

For a sample of this area, hike as close to the Colorado River gorge as practical until the summit of an exceptionally high sandstone dome is attained. There is a deep pothole at the top of this dome that is generally full of water, and the view from there of lower Bootlegger Canyon and the river gorge is outstanding. For more variety, make the return hike back from the rivergorge rimlands, avoiding the brushy, cattle-trampled meadows beyond the slickrock dome area.

The fourth and largest slickrock area in this segment of the Poison Spider - Gold Bar Rims area is along and below its highest rim, which looms above one end of Moab Valley. Here, the steep slopes along the rim of the Colorado River gorge and downslope from the high rim that overlooks Moab Valley, are Navajo Sandstone that has been shaped into an angled maze of domes, small canyons, ledges wide and narrow, giant potholes full of water and all the other shapes and forms that eons of erosion can create from this pale-hued aeolian sandstone.

In the northwestern part of this area, two canyons slice deeply through the Navajo and into the underlying Kayenta sandstone layers.

Rivergorge rim views from Poison Spider Mesa

The larger of these is Bootlegger Canyon, into which the railroad tunnel emerges near its lower end. Spectacular Corona Arch stands on a rock terrace high above the tracks, near a big pothole arch called Bowtie.

The other deep canyon is unnamed on topographic maps but for the purposes of this book has been named Calico Canyon. Hikers who reach the upper drainage of Calico Canyon, above its spectacular pouroff into the deep lower canyon, will find two large caves eroded into one of its low walls. Beyond these caves to the west, a lofty ridge of Navajo Sandstone separates Calico and Bootlegger canyons. From near the tip of this ridge, hikers can look down and across the canyon at Corona and Bowtie arches, from high above these beautiful spans.

Altogether, it would be easy and highly rewarding to spend days or even weeks exploring the complexities of the immense Poison Spider - Gold Bar Rim sandstone wilderness. Although several branching ORV trails penetrate the area, these are barely visible most places and do not detract from the slickrock wilderness-hiking experience. They are, however, essential for practical access into an area that is defined by sheer sandstone cliffs on all sides.

WATER-LIFE

My wife and I were hiking along one of the rimlands of Poison Spider Mesa, enjoying the splendid view across the deep Colorado River gorge of similar massive, rounded Navajo Sandstone fins and domes on Amasa Back, a slender peninsula formed by an elongated loop of the river.

We had just descended into one of the several hanging canyons that eons of erosion had cut into the massive slickrock rim, to examine more closely the canyon's intricate system of alcoves, its immense undercut pouroff, and its complex, water-carved drainage line, and were ascending the far slope, following the path of least resistance up a small subsidiary drainage, with its shallow, dry, stair-step potholes cut into solid rock.

As usual, I was plodding ahead, with my attention split between scouting the best route up out of the small canyon and studying its intricate beauty, while my wife was tagging along a few yards behind. With no need to look for a practical route up the steep slickrock slope, she was seeing more than I was at the moment, so spotted a singular phenomenon that I had missed -- an odd pothole, a very odd pothole.

There, on a tilted, smoothly-weathered slope of solid sandstone was a typical series of circular, shallow potholes, the kind that take centuries to form in such an arid environment. All were perfectly normal -- empty of everything but a few grains of sand -- except for one that was only slightly deeper, perhaps ten inches or a foot altogether.

And in this eccentric pothole was a miniature -- well, call it a swamp. But a swamp, in a four-foot sandstone pothole less than a foot deep? In an arid high-desert setting? Incredible!

But there it was, a tiny plant community whose dominant plant-life was a thick cluster of cat-tails, with their bulbous, water-holding roots. The scant water the pothole collected each rare time it rained was gone, evaporated into the desiccated desert air, yet the cat-tails were still alive, if not thriving. Dried, brown stalks taller than the rest of the short, slender leaves indicated that the water-loving plants had bloomed earlier and formed their fat, cylindrical heads, but these were now gone, perhaps broken off and blown away, perhaps eaten by some hungry herbivore. But what kind of desert creature eats cat-tail heads?

We stood marveling at this high-desert oddity -- a slickrock pothole swamp -- for several minutes, musing over how it might have come to be in this unlikely place, then climbed on up to the higher rimlands without a good answer between us. One more desert mystery, of the kind we encounter almost every time we take a slickrock hike -- the kind that fascinates, intrigues, tantalizes, excites, inspires and challenges, yet also irritates because there are no easy, apparent answers.

Farther along, at the summit of the highest sandstone dome on the rim, we found a very deep, very large, steep-walled pothole eight or ten feet wide, and perhaps as deep -- we couldn't tell. It was almost full of clear, cold water. The area of rock that drained into this pool was negligible, a thousandth of that which drained into and through the micro-swamp with its cat-tails, yet this one was full of water -- a deep, almost cylindrical lake of water, high atop a massive, rounded dome of white Navajo Sandstone. And while it hosted no large water-plants, it doubtless contained its own thriving ecosystem of microscopic plant and animal life. Water in this desiccated, high-desert country, whether ephemeral or enduring, always does. In this environment, water is too precious to waste even a drop, so where a drop exists, so does life, of one kind or another.

The big pothole that became Little Arch, Poison Spider Mesa

NAME - UPPER SEVENMILE CANYON

TYPE - area

ROCK - Kayenta and Wingate sandstones

USE - hiking and limited biking

GUIDEBOOK & MAP - any highway map of southeastern Utah

VEHICLE - off-road vehicle

ACCESS

Drive north from Moab on U.S. 191, then west on Utah 313, as shown on any map of southeastern Utah. After Utah 313 has climbed out of Sevenmile Canyon and traveled for about 3 miles beyond the summit of the switchbacks, turn left onto an off-road vehicle trail a few hundred yards before the paved road ascends a steep, curving grade. Stay on this ORV trail as it crosses a sandy meadow and descends into lower country, keeping left at trail junctions.

Hikers should park anywhere just before the trail angles steeply left down a sandy slope to cross a small canyon. Bikers should continue on this trail to just beyond the small canyon, where it first reaches the slickrock benchlands adjacent to this South Fork of Sevenmile Canyon.

DESCRIPTION

This small but interesting area consists of the upper drainage of the South Fork of Sevenmile Canyon plus its northern rimlands. Part of the canyon-bottom is slickrock, and part is the sediments normal to such relatively level canyons. This area is close to a paved highway and is thus accessible year around, except during exceptionally snowy winters.

Bikers can explore the broad Kayenta slickrock benchland above the canyon. An area more than a mile long and several hundred feet wide is bikable. Adventurous bikers can try to travel the canyon rimlands for another mile or so to the distant sandstone point that marks the junction of the north and south forks of Sevenmile. An ORV trail climbs from that area to Utah 313, reaching it near the top of the steep switchbacks.

202

Hikers should descend into the canyon as close to the indicated parking site as possible. A small tributary canyon to the south gives steep but easy access to the main canyon. On down the canyon, a side-canyon to the south is worth exploring, at least to where it ends in a water-carved alcove and a large pool of water.

The hike down the main drainage ends where it plunges over a sheer drop of about 100 feet to a lower level. It is possible to climb out of the canyon at this point by ascending the steep slope to the left of the drop. This permits the exploration of the complex Kayenta sandstone rimlands on the return hike. Hikers can also explore farther downcanyon, but not entirely on slickrock, to the picturesque canyon confluence, then back to their vehicle, thus making a longer round-trip hike.

Slitwindow Arch, near trail to Upper Sevenmile Canyon

NAME - WHITE RIM

TYPE - route

ROCK - Cutler-White Rim member

USE - hiking only

GUIDEBOOK & MAP - *Canyon Country* OFF-ROAD VEHICLE TRAILS - Island Area and matching map

VEHICLE - off-road vehicle

ACCESS

Drive onto the White Rim ORV trail in Canyonlands National Park from either end, as described in the referenced book and map.

From its east end, drive this trail until it ascends from lower country to the White Rim, then continue to its junction with the lower end of the Shafer Trail.

From its west end, descend into the Green River gorge, then continue downriver to where the first White Rim sandstone appears along the river bank.

DESCRIPTION

The White Rim ORV trail travels for many miles along the base of the soaring cliffs of Island-in-the-Sky, staying on the broad, level benchlands created there by the shelving White Rim sandstone, and cutting across the many large peninsulas created by the more erosion-resistant White Rim rock. The wildly meandering rim of this impressive rock layer is many times longer than the ORV trail itself, and provides countless spectacular views into the vividly colorful lower country that are not visible from the vehicle trail itself.

Beginning from either end of this long, meandering ORV trail, it is possible and quite rewarding to hike directly along the outermost rim of the White Rim benchland, as the ORV trail takes short-cuts. This kind of hiking is best done in segments, with support from an off-road vehicle left on the road while hiking each bypassed slickrock peninsula.

White Rim -- aerial photo

Since this is a National Park, and a ranger-patrolled vehicle trail, it would be best to tell park rangers in advance of plans to do this kind of vehicle-supported slickrock exploring. Even then a note should be left on the vehicle's windshield mentioning that it is not in trouble but parked for hiking.

Exploring any significant stretch of the White Rim by hiking can take many days, necessitating camping along the way at one of the designated camping areas. Reservations are required for these during periods of heavier park visitation.

Although the scenery below the entire White Rim is outstanding, if a choice must be made, the central stretch of the trail, that to the south, west and east of Grandview Point and Junction Butte, is the most spectacular, with the long rim around Monument Basin being a highlight.

NAME - C O U R T H O U S E - S E V E N M I L E R I M S

TYPE - area

ROCK - Navajo Sandstone and Entrada-Dewey Bridge Member

USE - hiking and biking

GUIDEBOOK & MAP - *Canyon Country* OFF-ROAD VEHICLE TRAILS - Island Area and matching map

VEHICLE - off-road vehicle

ACCESS

Drive north from Moab on U.S. 191 then west on the Monitor & Merrimac ORV trail, as described in the referenced book and map. Continue on this trail to the broad, flat slickrock area between the massive Monitor & Merrimac buttes.

Merrimac Butte

208

DESCRIPTION

The slickrock hiking and biking from the described access point is freelance, but can be done in several directions and cover several distinct but interconnected areas.

The first and closest area is the wide terrace of sandstone that surrounds immense Merrimac Butte, and its extension of rolling slickrock domes toward the west. The stair-step levels of red-hued Entrada-Dewey Bridge member around the immense monolith, just above its white Navajo Sandstone base, are also worth exploring.

Similarly, the slickrock terraces and jutting peninsulas that surround the smaller Monitor, especially those along its southern side, make fascinating hiking and offer outstandingly scenic views across the Sevenmile Canyon system and on south.

Although it requires some hiking across stretches of sandy, brushy meadow, or driving the rough and often obscure ORV trail loop that goes through the area, the third and largest segment of hikable and bikable slickrock in this general area is farther northeast along the Sevenmile Canyon rim, high above paved Utah 313, then northward along the high rimlands overlooking U.S. 191 and Arches National Park to the east.

Along the Sevenmile Canyon rim, watch for and explore a small but exceptionally colorful hanging canyon that plunges into Sevenmile and, where the cliffline angles northward, sample the spectacular 360-degree view from the still higher promontory that caps the ridge there.

The view from the eastern ridgeline of Courthouse Pasture is outstanding. Beyond the highway at the base of the soaring cliff, the entire upper Courthouse Canyon complex is discernible. Beyond that, the myriad fantastic geologic shapes and landforms of Arches National Park can be seen in stereoscopic detail. The soaring peaks of the La Sal Mountains dominate the southeastern skyline, while to the east the northern nose of the Uncompahgre Plateau looms on the distant horizon.

Along this stretch of slickrock rimland, Uranium Arch straddles a pouroff in a shallow drainage in the white sandstone a hundred yards back from the rim. The heavy bulldozing and drilling apparent along and back from the rim was done by uranium miners who were trying to relocate the ore vein they were mining in the shafts near the base of the cliff, those that are apparent from the highway below. It will be centuries before this scarring of public land is healed by nature.

Uranium Arch

NAME - SHORT CANYON HIGHLANDS

TYPE - area

ROCK - Navajo Sandstone

USE - hiking only

GUIDEBOOK & MAP - *Canyon Country* HIGHWAY TOURING and any highway map of southeastern Utah

VEHICLE - highway vehicle

ACCESS

Drive north from Moab on U.S. 191, then down the Colorado River on Utah 279, as described in the referenced book and map. Park in a grassy pulloff beside the road at the mouth of a heavily vegetated canyon about 9-1/2 miles from U.S. 191. The 1/2 mile route to the elevated, hikable slickrock area between this canyon and the next one downriver begins here.

This limited but beautiful and varied area provides an excellent introduction to typical Navajo Sandstone slickrock hiking that is easily accessible to highway vehicles and close to Moab and the river gorge camping areas beside Utah 279.

DESCRIPTION

Short Canyon, a name that does not appear on maps, is only about 1/2 mile long, heavily vegetated and ends in a spectacular pouroff amphitheater that is exceptionally beautiful in late October, when fall colors prevail. To explore the Short Canyon slickrock area, enter the canyon by climbing the cattle-control fence at the righthand wall of the canyon, then stay close to this wall for easy progress until forced into the sandy drainage line by dense vegetation. Continue up the canyon to the immense, soaring alcove at its end.

The damage to this erstwhile lovely canyon's vegetation and spring-fed pools is from the periodic short-term use of the canyon for grazing cattle. Even if this obvious misuse of public land were to be discontinued, decades would pass before the former natural beauty of the canyon was restored by nature. Hikers who object to this senseless destruction of natural beauty and public land values might consider addressing their concerns to the nearest BLM office and their elected representatives in Washington.

Near the upper end of the canyon, a ledge blasted from the righthand canyon wall permits ascent to an elevated wedge of land that can be reached no other way. Unfortunately, this highly scenic stretch of slickrock, ancient river gravel and sandy hillocks is also used and abused by cattle, and is hence somewhat scarred and its vegetation damaged, but the views down into the canyon and river gorge from its slickrock rims are excellent. Rockhounds will find a wide variety of collectible specimens in the immense mounds of river gravel, which contain rock from all the terrain through which the Colorado River flows.

The main area of slickrock, between the canyons, is reached by hiking to the large plunge-pool at the head of Short Canyon, then climbing upward to the left on the sandstone slopes there. This route provides easy access to a large area of multi-level slickrock that contains several large caverns, still more hills of gravel deposited there before the river cut to its present depth, and the sandstone rimlands of the both canyons. The area is limited and defined by the two canyons, the sheer wall of the river's inner gorge and still higher walls of Navajo Sandstone farther back from the river.

After exploring the immense highlands between the two canyons, return to the highway by the same route.

Corona and Bowtie arches from Short Canyon Highlands

A CALICO CANYON

Winter days are short, so we choose smaller places to explore then, places we have been saving up for just such times.

We generally hike on slickrock in the winter, but not always. Sometimes we decide to hike on another kind of "slickrock" that is almost as hard as sandstone and truly slick -- the ice that builds up in spring-wetted canyons during the colder months of winter.

The unnamed canyon we picked to explore that bright but cold day penetrated the great mass of Navajo Sandstone that was the base of Poison Spider Mesa along the Colorado River. It was easily accessible from the paved road there, Utah 279, so we didn't have to use our off-road vehicle for access.

We shrugged on our packs -- my wife's had our lunch, mine our camera equipment -- and headed up the canyon. At first it was not much to see. It had been severely disturbed by the past construction of a rail-road tunnel and embankment, and was evidently used by cattle some time during the year. It was a mess, and that was probably why it was not used much by hikers -- and why we had not sampled it before.

But recent studies of a topographic map had told me that the canyon had hidden promise, so we had decided to tolerate the mess "civilization" had made of the canyon's mouth, in order to see what mysteries were hidden in its upper reaches.

For a short distance we scrambled through a heavy thicket of dead cane-grasses beside a steep slope of the railroad embankment, then through a frozen swamp of still denser growth into the branch of the forked canyon that we wanted to explore. The railroad dominated the other fork, before entering its tunnel.

Around the first bend of the deepening canyon, as we left the thick reeds of the lower canyon, we entered a land of enchantment! Seeping springs, and a tiny stream that was probably a bare trickle during warmer months, had built an icy wonderland in the canyon bottom. A few inches of snow transformed the surrounding brush, trees and rock walls and ledges into a fairyland of white, crystalline beauty. The winter-shadowed canyon was bright with reflected and re-reflected light -- light that turned somber winter hues into a bright kaleidoscope of vivid color.

The stream course in the canyon bottom that cascaded down a series of slickrock plunge-pools was a great linear mass of artfully sculpt-ed white ice, a challenging walkway of slippery "slickrock" that offered a seemingly-easy route on up the canyon. The awesome canyon walls were vast draperies of reddish, mineral-stained rock, red-brown desert varnish and black lichens.

As we paused to admire this fantastic scene just a few yards beyond the mess of the lower canyon, my wife muttered " - calico, the canyon is calico-colored, red and white and black, like our calico-cat." The name was perfect and it stuck. We have since then called that hidden place "Calico Canyon."

On up the canyon, its walls grew higher still, until the sky was almost gone. The frozen streamlet gave easy but slippery passage, but a deer trail through the brush was better, with no chance of breaking through the icy crust into unfrozen water.

The head of the mile-long canyon was an enormous, soaring amphitheater, with row after row of parallel seep-lines up its vast water-sculpted curvature. The vegetation that normally grew in such seep-lines -- ferns, columbines and other water-loving plants -- was dormant, but the seeps were not. The slowly dripping water had frozen as it seeped from each horizontal line, building row above parallel row of gigantic icicles six to eight feet in length. These rows stretched for a hundred feet or more around the curvature of the amphitheater wall. Other nearby seeps had constructed great luminescent ice-walls that cascaded down over sandstone ledges to the canyon floor. The place was a crystalline palace, a gigantic, enchanted sandstone alcove that was a combination of the best that canyon country had to offer, melded with the best that winter could produce -- an incomparable place of chromatic beauty, of color and light.

The following spring we explored the next canyon over, one still shorter which we dubbed "Short Canyon." Its beauty was marred for its entire length by cattle, but we found at its end a way up onto the elevated, isolated slickrock peninsula that separates the two canyons.

From the rim of Calico Canyon it still looked inviting, and we eventually found a hazardous way down into it from that rim, but somehow the warm-season canyon lacked the enchantment it had held for us in mid-winter. It was green and lovely, but not so calico-colored, with the ice and snow gone.

But we remember it -- we remember it the way it was on that cold winter day.

NAME - UPPER SEVENMILE SOUTH FORK

TYPE - route

ROCK - Kayenta Sandstone

USE - hiking only

GUIDEBOOK & MAP - *Canyon Country* OFF-ROAD VEHICLE TRAILS - Island Area and matching map

VEHICLE - off-road vehicle or highway vehicle

ACCESS

For access using any kind of vehicle, drive north from Moab on U.S. 191, west on Utah 313, then east on graded dirt Arths Pasture Road, as described in the referenced book and map. About 2-3/4 miles from the pavement, watch for an obscure ORV trail to the left that shortly drops steeply into one upper end of the south fork of Sevenmile Canyon. Highway vehicles must park here, but off-road vehicles can travel this trail for about 3/4 of a mile to where it crosses the canyon bottom and park there.

DESCRIPTION

The general route of this relatively short but interesting slickrock hike is downcanyon, and hikers will find a variety of ways to accomplish this, a few of which quite probably will not turn out to be practical. Because of frequent pouroffs, it is not possible to simply hike down the canyon's drainage, but steady progress can be made along the terraced Kayenta Sandstone layers of either rim.

In between some of the numerous pouroffs along the drainage, it is worth descending to the canyon floor and exploring back up to the undercut pouroffs, although with caution because subsurface moisture allows poison oak to thrive along some stretches of the wash. In other parts of the drainage, water has carved deep potholes that generally contain water during the wetter months. A few are deep enough to retain water all year long.

After about 1 mile, a very high pouroff prevents further progress except along the lofty rim of the much deeper canyon. Here, the canyon below the pouroff is wet from seeping springs and lush with vegetation, but inaccessible from above. A short hike along the left rim of the deeper canyon to a shallow tributary drainage is worthwhile, because near the lip of the drainage pouroff a sizable hole has formed in the roof of the seep-cavern below, forming a natural bridge of sorts. For still more Kayenta Sandstone hiking, continue along the terraces in either direction below the major pouroff, along the cliffline of the deeper canyon.

For further non-slickrock exploring in this area, hike upcanyon from the ORV trail. This hike is especially nice during early spring months, when wildflowers are in bloom along the canyon bottom. Because the surrounding terrain is somewhat tilted, the canyon becomes much deeper toward its upper end. There is an immense, open-topped cavern called Aviary Arch on the right side of the canyon, and another smaller but interesting span just above the end of the left of two short forks in the canyon's upper end.

For hikers who have not driven down into the canyon, it is possible to climb out of the upper canyon to its white slickrock rim via a broad side-bay in the canyon, then on south to Arths Pasture Road, not far from the ORV access trail junction. The canyon's slickrock rim in this vicinity is interesting to explore, and offers fine views down into the canyon.

Winter hiking, Monitor & Merrimac buttes in the distance

STEEP

We were sitting in the welcome shade of a slickrock alcove, after having hiked across slickrock for a half-mile or so, waiting near one picturesque leg of Moab's Slickrock Bike Trail -- waiting for some bikers to come by so I could photograph them against the spectacular background I had chosen.

It was a warm day, but the Trail was busy with energetic bikers, some alone, others in groups, and a few man-woman pairs. We watched, as one such pair crossed the bright expanse of slickrock below and to our left. I got my camera ready for when they would cross the chosen background slightly below us.

As they approached the slickrock grade that had to be ascended to reach our level, they momentarily went out of sight, but we knew where that had to go, since we could see the paint-marked route from where we sat.

Then, abruptly, the man rose into view, pedaling furiously -- but where was his partner? I needed them together for the picture! Then she showed up, too far behind him for a picture, complaining loudly --

" -- I HATE steep! You KNOW I hate steep!"

We smiled and waved cheerfully to the two happy bikers as they passed near us, even though we were having great difficulty choking back impolite laughter at the little domestic scene!

I did get a useful picture, however, because the bike route made a sharp loop nearby and then crossed my chosen background again, in an even more spectacular perspective, and by then the two were separated by just the right amount. I put this picture in my book, **Canyon Country MOUNTAIN BIKING,** on the bottom of page 27.

And ever since then, my wife and I seldom climb a steep slickrock slope without one of us saying --

"Steep! You KNOW I hate steep!"

LA SALS AREA

This geographic area is defined by the Colorado River in the north, U.S.191 in the west, Utah 46 and Colorado 90 in the south, and the Dolores River in the east. The perimeter highways and the roads and off-road vehicle trails within the area are described in another *Canyon Country* guidebook and matching map. These are listed by title in each area description and on the inside-back cover of this book.

NAME - MILL CREEK TRIANGLE

TYPE - area

ROCK - Navajo Sandstone

USE - hiking only

GUIDEBOOK & MAP - *Canyon Country* **OFF-ROAD VEHICLE TRAILS - Arches & La Sals Areas** and matching map

VEHICLE - off-road vehicle

ACCESS

Drive southeast from Moab on Murphy Lane, then east on the Mill Creek Canyon ORV trail to the summit of the pass just before this trail first descends into the Mill Creek drainage, as described in the referenced book and map. Continue on this trail as it descends into the canyon bottom, travels upstream with several fordings, then climbs steeply out of the canyon. At each of the next several main trail junctions, go left. The trail eventually reaches relatively level but much higher terrain, and heads northeastwardly into the heart of the Mill Creek Triangle. Park wherever the hiking looks good, then continue on foot.

As an alternate but much longer approach, drive southeast from Moab on Spanish Valley Road, then drive the Mill Creek Canyon ORV trail from its southern end via Flat Pass to the Mill Creek Triangle spur, as described in the referenced guidebook and map.

DESCRIPTION

The Mill Creek Triangle is an elevated peninsula of Navajo Sandstone that lies between Mill Creek Canyon and its main tributary, the North Fork of Mill Creek Canyon. These two deep, sheer-walled canyons severely limit access to the Triangle from the creeks themselves, allowing practical access only via a spur of the Mill Creek Canyon ORV trail.

The Triangle is a maze of typical Navajo Sandstone domes and fins several square miles in size. Hikers can get an introduction to the area's highlights by circumnavigating the peninsula as nearly as practical to the two canyon rims, thus affording spectacular views down into both the canyons and their many tributaries, with views of their flowing streams, beaver dams, cottonwood groves, cascades, waterfalls and grassy meadows.

One of the several smaller canyons that spur from the North Fork has immense Otho Natural Bridge in its upper end. Hikers who can navigate using a topographic map can reach the canyon rim above this massive natural span. It is shown as "Natural Arch" on the 7-1/2 minute U.S.G.S. quadrangle map titled "Rill Creek, Utah."

From where the ORV access trail ends between slickrock fins, facing a higher, flat-topped promontory of younger deposits, the very steep nature of the sandstone fins below the promontory makes it is necessary to hike down into lower terrain before continuing on toward the main body of the peninsula. Even then, this area is so large in scale, so vertical and so drastically eroded, that there simply is no easy and obvious hiking route. This makes the area especially challenging to hikers who appreciate the special nature of canyon country slickrock hiking on Navajo Sandstone.

In compensation for the difficulties, the views in all directions from almost anywhere in the Mill Creek Triangle area are outstanding, with breathtaking canyons below, the lofty La Sal Mountains to the southeast, Moab Valley to the south and west, and the sandstone wilderness of the Sand Flats to the east.

NAME - PORCUPINE RIM

TYPE - route

ROCK - Kayenta Sandstone

USE - hiking only

GUIDEBOOK & MAP - *Canyon Country* OFF-ROAD VEHICLE TRAILS - **Arches & La Sals Areas** and matching map

VEHICLE - highway vehicle to one access point, off-road vehicle to the other

ACCESS

For the highway vehicle access point, drive up the Sand Flats ORV trail from Moab to the beginning of the Porcupine Rim ORV trail, then hike that vehicle trail to its first approach to Porcupine Rim. Off-road vehicles can also use this access by driving to the rim approach, or by continuing on the Sand Flats Road for about 2-1/4 miles beyond the water tanks that mark the beginning of the Porcupine Rim ORV trail, then going left on a 1/2-mile spur ORV trail to the Porcupine Rim ORV trail and on to Porcupine Rim.

DESCRIPTION

Porcupine Rim is the lofty, tilted southwestern rim of spectacular Castle Valley. Altogether, this rim is some twelve miles long, from where it emerges from slopes of the La Sal Mountains to where it reaches the Colorado River gorge, but much of this does not offer practical slickrock hiking.

At best, the Kayenta slickrock along the rim is intermittent, trees and brush slow progress and the rim is cut in many places by drainage lines that must be crossed.

In compensation for this difficult hiking, the views down into and across Castle Valley are magnificent and continually changing. The cliff falls sheer from the rim for some distance, then steep slopes of rubble and giant boulders continue on down to the valley floor in great sweeping curves.

In the uppermost part of the valley, an arm called Pinhook Valley was once the setting for an historic Indian massacre. Just down-canyon from there, symmetrical Round Mountain stands alone, a remnant of ancient intrusive volcanic activity. Historic Porcupine Ranch is nearby, almost directly below the rim.

On down Castle Valley, recent human developments dominate the valley floor, while its far side is defined by the lofty peninsula of Adobe Mesa, soaring Castle Tower, the butte that ends with the tall monoliths, The Priest and Nuns, and Parriott Mesa. Parts of verdant Professor Valley are visible beyond Castle Tower, as is the Colorado River in the distance as it winds through the vast open expanse of Richardson Amphitheater.

Porcupine Rim and the La Sal Mountains -- aerial photo

226

From much of the rim, the complex Negro Bill canyon system, Moab Valley and the vast redrock wilderness beyond are visible to the south and west. The La Sal Mountains dominate the horizon to the east, while the high rimlands of Top-of-the-World and the Uncompahgre Uplift are visible to the northeast. On clear days, the distant Book Cliffs can be seen to the north.

The vegetation along Porcupine Rim is the upper Pinyon-Juniper community. Since it has largely been undisturbed by cattle and various destructive "range-management" practices, it provides hikers a good look at what much of the region looked like prior to the arrival of modern man and his domestic livestock.

NAME - RILL CANYON

TYPE - route

ROCK - Kayenta and Wingate sandstones

USE - hiking only

GUIDEBOOK & MAP - *Canyon Country* OFF-ROAD VEHICLE TRAILS - Arches & La Sals Areas and matching map

VEHICLE - off-road vehicle or high-clearance highway vehicle

ACCESS

Drive up the Sand Flats ORV trail from Moab. About 6-1/2 miles from where the trail branches from Mill Creek Road, watch for an ORV trail that angles to the right toward an abandoned oil-drill site. With careful driving, low-geared, high-clearance highway vehicles can negotiate this trail to where the hiking begins. Stay on this trail for about 1 mile, as it travels generally southeastward toward the La Sal Mountains, then park where it first reaches the rim overlooking Rill Canyon.

DESCRIPTION

Rill Canyon is about 5 miles long. Its head is 4 miles upstream from this access point, and it ends where it joins the North Fork of Mill Creek about 1 mile downstream of this point. There are only two practical access routes to the canyon within its 5-mile length. One access is here, the other is from the Sand Flats ORV trail as it skirts along the steep slopes of upper Rill Canyon, about 1/2 mile from the canyon head.

It is also possible, of course, to enter and leave Rill Canyon from its confluence with the North Fork of Mill Creek. Although there is a way to climb down into and out of North Fork from the canyon rimlands about 2 miles cross-country from this access point, the route between the rim and the canyon floor of North Fork is not readily apparent or easily described, and is hence not recommended without a knowledgeable guide.

There are several ways to hike Rill Canyon, depending on how much time is available, whether some canyon-hiking other than on slickrock is tolerable and if a vehicle shuttle can be arranged. Two suggested hikes are described here, one largely on slickrock and fairly short, the other longer with some canyon-bottom rubble-scrambling. Both hikes begin from the described rim access point, and both require returning to this access point.

From the rim overlooking Rill Canyon, hike down the steep, eroded remnant of an ORV trail to the broad, sloping benchland that lies above the Rill Canyon inner gorge. Angle left across this benchland by any convenient route, then look for the easiest way down into the inner gorge, preferably just above a sharp turn in the creek.

229

For a short but rewarding one-day slickrock hike from the benchland, hike upstream for a few yards, to see a series of interesting grottoes cut into the solid sandstone, then head back downstream to Rill's confluence with the North Fork of Mill Creek. Explore a few hundred yards up North Fork, then return back upcanyon, leaving the inner gorge anywhere practical below the vehicle access point. Return to the rim via the same old ORV trail used for the descent.

For a much longer one-day hike, continue up Rill Canyon for about 2 miles. The mouth of rugged Burkholder Draw is about 1/2 mile above the described inner gorge access point. Continue up Rill to anywhere beyond a series of steep slickrock cascades with pools and a "rill" of water fed by a number of seeps from the steep canyon walls, then hike back downstream to its confluence with North Fork and return to the access point.

Rill Canyon, from just above the access point into the inner gorge near the hairpin curve, to it confluence with North Fork is largely slickrock along its bottom. During the wetter seasons, a trickling stream flows down a series of rock slides, cascades and plunges, through a number of lovely slickrock pools, some of them large enough for a cooling dip, before it joins the perennially flowing creek of North Fork. Hikers who go any distance up North Fork should beware of the poison oak that grows along some stretches of the canyon narrows above the Rill-North Fork confluence.

Although Rill Canyon is nice for hiking, up or down, at any time of the year, this isolated canyon is truly delightful during the early spring, when water is flowing at its best and desert wildflowers in full bloom grace the rock-terraced stream banks. Autumn offers a different spectrum of wildflowers and some colorful fall leaves, but Rill Creek is generally dry then.

The upper 3-1/2 miles of the isolated canyon are partly slickrock, and partly canyon-wall rubble, with trees and other vegetation making hiking more difficult along some stretches. This is also true of the tributary canyon, Burkholder Draw. The upper canyon, however, is delightful in its own way. During the cold winter months, its many seeping springs create immense cascades of ice that sometimes last into late spring.

NAME - SAND FLATS

TYPE - areas

ROCK - Navajo Sandstone

USE - hiking and limited biking

GUIDEBOOK & MAP - *Canyon Country* OFF-ROAD VEHICLE TRAILS - **Arches & La Sals Areas** and matching map

VEHICLE - highway vehicle

ACCESS

Drive up the Sand Flats ORV trail from Mill Creek Road in Moab to any number of places where it is possible to hike from the road to nearby slickrock areas. This ORV trail is a paved, then graded dirt road, for its first 9 miles. The following descriptions are limited to areas adjacent to this stretch of the trail. Beyond the spring-fed tanks that are on the narrow ridge between Rill and Negro Bill canyons, this trail becomes too rough and steep for highway vehicles. Several sample areas and their access points within the first 9 miles are described in the following paragraphs.

Mill Creek Rims

232

DESCRIPTIONS

MILL CREEK RIMS AREA

Drive up the Sand Flats trail to just beyond where it climbs steeply into higher terrain, then travels near the sandstone rim above the local dump. Park anywhere near where the road turns sharply left, then hike southeasterly up into the slickrock fins straight ahead. Stay as close to the rim of the valley as practical, changing fins only when forced to.

In about 1 mile, the deep gorge of the North Fork of Mill Creek Canyon will appear far below. Descend as far as possible by hiking down one of the sandstone fins there, then skirt left to Pocket Arch, a delightful, well-hidden span above a seeping spring between two immense slickrock fins.

Ascend the fin beside the arch, then continue hiking as close to the rim of North Fork as practical. By taking a number of detours around slot canyons that penetrate the rim, and one major tributary canyon, it is possible to hike the North Fork rimlands all the way to within sight of this canyon's confluence with Rill Canyon, but some stretches of this challenging hike will not be on slickrock.

To return from this route, either retrace the outbound route, or hike generally northward from almost anywhere to the Sand Flats trail, which is within 1 mile of this route anywhere. The described route offers access along the way to several major areas of slickrock fins and domes well worth exploring.

NEGRO BILL CANYON RIMS AREAS

Drive up the Sand Flats trail to just beyond where it climbs steeply into higher terrain, then travels near the sandstone rim above the local dump. Park anywhere near where the road turns sharply left, then climb up the first fin in the curve of the trail. Continue fin-hiking in a northwesterly direction until it is necessary to drop down between fins and follow an old ORV trail that shortly goes through a fence line. From there, angle across the sloping meadows toward the masses of slickrock visible to the north.

This route provides easy access into the several square miles of slickrock wilderness defined by Moab Valley, the Colorado River gorge and Negro Bill Canyon, an area sculptured by eons of erosion into a three-dimensional maze that is a challenge to explore, yet is quite close to Moab. Loops of the Moab Slickrock Bike Trail penetrate this slickrock area in places.

For access to another even larger such area, drive up the Sand Flats trail to just beyond the entrance to the Moab Slickrock Bike Trail, then hike northward across the immense expanse of slickrock there toward another segment of Negro Bill Canyon. From the rimlands of the canyon, hike generally upcanyon, exploring the large fins and domes of slickrock in the vicinity. Some hiking on soils and sand will be necessary between expanses of sandstone, but these continue upcanyon for several miles, almost to where Negro Bill and Rill canyons are separated by a narrow ridge traveled by the Sand Flats trail.

This intermittent area of Navajo Sandstone affords continuous spectacular views down into deep and narrow Negro Bill Canyon and, at one point, offers hikers a route down into the canyon via a tributary canyon penetrated by an old cattle trail. There are lovely springs and pools with shady cottonwood trees part-way down this unnamed tributary canyon.

NOTE: the land just beyond the Slickrock Bike Trail is part of a Utah State "school section" that is subject to possible leasing and private development. If this occurs, hikers should continue up the Sand Flats trail to beyond the developed area, then hike toward Negro Bill Canyon from there.

Winter hiking, Negro Bill Canyon Rims

CENTRAL FINS AREA

Drive up the Sand Flats trail for about 2 miles beyond the start of the Slickrock Bike Trail, then explore the maze of sandstone fins and domes on either side of the trail. Here, again, the slickrock will be intermittent, but the number and variety of immense masses of slickrock makes this area worth exploring.

234

Part of the challenge in this area is trying to reach the tops of as many sandstone fins as possible, without taking hazardous routes. The slickrock in this area is much like the Navajo Sandstone in other areas in that it contains numerous fascinating caves, alcoves and potholes, plus a wide variety of erosional features, some inexplicable even to geologists.

The sandstone here also exhibits many curious variations of desert-aeolian cross-stratification and erosion, as well as numerous exposed cross-sections of the strange "petrified playas," or ancient desert dry-lakes, that occasionally contain the preserved foot tracks of prehistoric animals such as dinosaurs, amphibians and pterosaurs, or flying reptiles. Several such sites have already been reported to paleontologists.

Pocket Arch

PETRIFIED OASIS

I was tired of writing and needed a break, a chance to renew my sense of reality, my enthusiasm for life. Nothing could do that better than a hike in some new area of slickrock, but my wife was gone for the day, on a trip with her group of singing Sweet Adelines.

Since we rarely did anything alone, it would feel kind of different scrambling over some new extent of slickrock without her, but I needed the stretch, I needed to look at something besides a computer monitor.

I needed to look at distant cliffs and mountains through crystal-clear air. I yearned to gaze at twisted juniper trees and clustered barrel cactus and little sand-dune ecosystems circumscribed by solid rock and tiny, ancient natural bonsai trees growing in sandstone crevices and lots and lots of sandstone of all colors and shapes. I needed a hike in canyon country.

So I headed for our back yard, the Sand Flats area, the high, maze-like tableland defined by Moab-Spanish Valley, Castle Valley, the Colorado River gorge and the La Sal Mountain foothills -- some 90 square miles of defacto wilderness cut only by one graded dirt access road and a few faint ORV trails.

I drove up the Sand Flats Road, heading for an elevated, flat-topped slickrock mesa that I recalled seeing, one that we had not yet explored. Once there, I parked the car, hiked through a few yards of sparse pinyon-juniper forest, then started climbing the slickrock slopes at the base of the mesa.

The way up was rough, steep and not obvious, but fairly easy as slickrock hiking goes. At the upper rim, I paused for a breath then slowly started hiking counterclockwise around the rim of the mesa. It was not very large. Going all the way around might take an hour, at the rate I usually hiked through such varied and interesting terrain -- unless I found something of special interest, or the distant scenery grew even more enchanting than it was already. I did and it did.

I had barely started hiking along the broken, eroded slickrock rim of the mesa when I spotted an anomaly, something different, something odd, lying on a light-hued sandstone slope. I picked up the piece of rock for a closer look, to make certain of what I had found.

I was right. The small, inconspicuous rock was not just a piece of fragmented, decomposing sandstone, it was petrified wood. I was not really surprised, because in recent months we and friends of ours had been finding petrified wood within Navajo Sandstone many places, fossil trees where trees were not supposed to be. And here was still another such place, where trees had grown in an arid, desert environment some 170 million years ago.

236

Trees take water to grow, permanent water, and in deserts permanent water is generally called an "oasis." So, although geologists don't use the term, and still didn't officially recognize our recent discoveries of fossil trees in Navajo Sandstone, we had been calling such localities "petrified oases."

We called similar water-affected layers within the Navajo that did not have fossil tree remnants "petrified playas," since the Spanish term "playa" is commonly applied by geologists and others to the kind of broad, shallow ephemeral dry-lakes that are common to the desert Southwest.

And I had just discovered another petrified oasis -- perhaps. To verify my find, to prove that the petrified wood fragment had not come from some younger and higher stratum, I started looking for the origin of the petrified wood, the log from which it had eroded and its rock matrix. To do this I carefully traced the tiny, shallow drainage upward from where I had found the first piece of agatized wood, finding more every few feet.

After a short climb, I found still more. I was on the right trail. A few feet beyond the edge of the exposed slickrock and across a small blackbrush meadow, I found the petrified log, lying partly buried in sandy soil and decomposed into thousands of fragments, but still holding something of its original shape.

After examining the ancient log for a few moments, I scouted around the vicinity, looking for more petrified tree remnants. I found several, then decided to continue my hike around the perimeter of the mesa, where erosion had exposed the petrified oasis layer and where it would be easier to spot fossil tree remnants.

I found a few others along the same rim, then came to a sight that for the moment made me forget about ancient dead trees -- a breathtaking view down into a deep gorge, hundreds of feet deep, and almost directly below the rim on which I stood.

After a long pause to enjoy the view, I continued my search, but found no more "wood" until I reached the corner of the mesa that turned away from spectacular upper Negro Bill Canyon. There, another small log was exposed, but then I saw nothing further along that third rim of the rectangular mesa.

The fourth leg of my rim-perimeter hike was almost solid exposed sandstone slickrock, sloping or terraced toward a steep drop. And the slickrock was littered with petrified -- what? At first glance it looked like more of the petrified wood I had been finding. A few fragments were, but not all. Most were the agatized rock of fossil wood, but did not exhibit the typical grain-structure of wood. The grain, where it was visible at all, was twisted, warped, gnarled, like the grain of some trees, but somehow different. And the rock was dark, almost black, much darker than the wood I had been finding.

One huge mass of the dark material closely resembled a tree-stump. It even had an internal hollow that had filled with light brown mud before fossilizing, like a partially rotted tree-stump. Yet I couldn't be sure. What *was* this strange life that had been growing in a desert swamp, an isolated oasis?

After thinking long about what might thrive in a desert pool, I guessed it might be algae, the kind of green, slimy mass of hair-like stuff that often fills seeping springs and tiny streams even today. I had seen petrified algae elsewhere, so knew it could exist, but not with this strange color and texture.

I have since given samples of this petrified plantlife to a geologist, but have yet to hear what he determined. Another friend, a paleontologist, also examined a specimen, and tentatively agreed with my algae idea, but was not certain.

What was certain, that day of my hike alone up onto a slickrock mesa, was that I had once again found something new and exciting, another canyon country mystery to solve -- and a place that I could hardly wait to share with my wife. Which I did, a few days later.

NAME-UPPER NEGRO BILL CANYON

TYPE - route

ROCK - Kayenta and Wingate sandstones

USE - hiking only

GUIDEBOOK & MAP - *Canyon Country* OFF-ROAD VEHICLE TRAILS - **Arches & La Sals Areas** and matching map

VEHICLE - off-road vehicles or others with additional hiking

ACCESS

Drive up the Sand Flats trail to either access route to the Porcupine Rim ORV trail. Off-road vehicles can drive this trail to where it crosses the upper Negro Bill Canyon drainage. Those with low-geared, high-clearance highway vehicles can drive to the upper access to the Porcupine Rim ORV trail, then hike it about 3/4 mile to the Negro Bill Canyon drainage. Those with standard highway vehicles can sample this slickrock hiking area by driving to the first access to the Porcupine Rim ORV trail, where spring-fed water tanks stand on a narrow ridge between Negro Bill and Rill canyons, then hiking about 2 miles on the ORV trail to where it crosses the Negro Bill Canyon drainage.

DESCRIPTION

This route can provide either a short sampler of Kayenta slick-rock hiking or an open-ended longer hike of any length.

The upper Negro Bill Canyon drainage is open and fairly shallow at first. It is set among typical pinyon-juniper forestland that during the warmer season hosts myriad wildflowers. The Kayenta Sandstone strata in this area were drastically tilted by the intrusion of the La Sal Mountains, but the drainage has cut downward even more steeply, creating a series of pouroffs that must be bypassed. Hike down the intricately eroded slickrock drainage line wherever possible, leaving it only as necessary to get around and below these pouroffs.

The first such ledge is within a hundred yards or so of where the ORV trail crosses the drainage, and there are others at regular intervals. While it is possible to bypass each of the several pouroff ledges and continue on down Negro Bill Canyon, the hikable slickrock in the drainage ends after about 1/2 mile.

From that point, slickrock hikers have two options: either return to the ORV trail, or continue to hike along the Kayenta Sandstone ledges on the right side of the rapidly deepening canyon. With care, persistence and considerable energy, it is possible to continue scrambling along the Kayenta ledges that make up the rimlands of upper Negro Bill Canyon for many miles, skirting around the tributary drainages that develop, and traveling the wild and broken terrain that lies between this deep canyon and higher Porcupine Rim to the northeast, which is the upper edge of picturesque Castle Valley.

240

Hikers who might wish to take a loop route can continue down the ledgy rim of Negro Bill Canyon as far as desired, then climb upward toward Porcupine Rim and return to their vehicle via the ORV trail that closely parallels this lofty rim.

From here on it's ledge-hiking

MAZE AREA

This geographic area is defined by the Green and Colorado rivers in the east and by arbitrary boundaries in the north and west that include all of the land in that area that is under National Park Service administration, including Canyonlands National Park and Glen Canyon National Recreation Area.

The perimeter highways and the roads and off-road vehicle trails within the area are described in another *Canyon Country* guidebook and matching map. These are listed by title in each area description and on the inside-back cover of this book.

Almost all of the hikable slickrock within the Maze Area is either White Rim Sandstone or Cedar Mesa Sandstone, both of them members of the Cutler Formation. Since most of the Maze Area in which these sandstones occur is within Canyonlands National Park, and these areas are so extensive there, only two specific areas are described as examples, one for each type of slickrock.

Mountain bikers should take note that Park Service policy requires wheeled vehicles to stay on designated ORV trails. Although this means that slickrock biking is more limited than slickrock hiking in the Maze Area, just staying on the ORV trails within the lower elevations of the area provides bikers ample opportunity to sample the slickrock there.

The Maze

NAME - LAND OF STANDING ROCKS

TYPE - area

ROCK - Cutler-Cedar Mesa Sandstone member

USE - hiking, with biking only on established ORV trails

GUIDEBOOK & MAP - *Canyon Country* OFF-ROAD VEHICLE TRAILS - **Maze Area** and matching map

VEHICLE - off-road vehicle

ACCESS

Drive to the Hans Flat visitor contact station in the Maze Area via either the road from Green River or the road from Utah 24, as described in the referenced book and map, then descend into the lower region via the Big Ridge ORV trail and the Flint Trail. At the trail junction at the base of the Flint Trail switchbacks, go right on the Land of Standing Rocks ORV trail.

As an alternate access route, drive north from Utah 95 on the Hite Road, as described in the same book and map. At the four-way junction 30 miles from Utah 95, turn right onto one loop of the Land of Standing Rocks trail.

DESCRIPTION

The Land of Standing Rocks trail begins traveling on and through Cedar Mesa slickrock country as it rounds the head of Teapot Canyon, at the base of Teapot Rock. This red-and-white banded sandstone dominates the terrain from there to the trail's end, in an immense "city" of sandstone towers formed from the rock, just beyond a row of gigantic figures of the same rock called The Doll House.

Although the region surrounding this ORV trail is not solid slickrock, it is possible to hike out across great expanses of Cedar Mesa slickrock from almost anywhere along the trail beyond Teapot Canyon, and some of the marked hiking trails enter mazes of this slickrock, such as The Fins or Ernies Country to the south of the trail.

The Fins

To the north of the trail, a complex series of deeply-cut canyons define The Maze itself. Foot trails descend into and travel these canyons, but the canyon bottoms are slickrock only here and there. The canyon rimlands, however, are almost continuous slickrock, and hence make excellent slickrock hiking. For a sample of this kind of Maze Area hiking, drive the longer loop of the ORV trail to Chimney Rock, then take the designated hiking trail toward distant Petes Mesa. Freelance slickrock hiking on Cedar Mesa Sandstone from this trail, around the base of Petes Mesa and in the general vicinity, provides an excellent introduction to the area.

The sandstone highlands above Water, Shot and Jasper canyons and the South Fork of immense Horse Canyon, all to the north of the ORV trail, offer still more hiking on Cedar Mesa slickrock.

Land of Standing Rocks -- Jack Bickers photo

The Doll House

Trail to Petes Mesa

Land of Standing Rocks -- Jack Bickers photo

NAME - BIG WATER CANYON

TYPE - area

ROCK - Cutler-White Rim Sandstone member

USE - hiking, with biking only on established ORV trails

GUIDEBOOK & MAP - *Canyon Country* OFF-ROAD VEHICLE TRAILS - **Maze Area** and matching map

VEHICLE - off-road vehicle

ACCESS

Drive to the Hans Flat visitor contact station in the Maze Area via either the road from Green River or the road from Utah 24, as described in the referenced book and map, then descend into the lower region via the Big Ridge ORV trail and the Flint Trail. At the trail junction at the base of the Flint Trail switchbacks, continue straight ahead on the Maze Overlook ORV trail, then down into the lower country on the same trail.

As an alternate access route, drive north from Utah 95 on the Hite Road, as described in the same book and map. At the four-way junction 30 miles from Utah 95, continue ahead on the Land of Standing Rocks ORV trail as it climbs to travel the higher benchlands and end at the trail junction at the base of the Flint Trail. Go right there on the Maze Overlook ORV trail.

Tar seeps, near Maze Overlook trail

DESCRIPTION

Within 2 miles, the Maze Overlook ORV trail has dropped into lower terrain and reached White Rim Sandstone country. It continues at this level for about another 12 miles, to where it ends at the Maze Overlook. About 9 miles from the trail's beginning at the base of the Flint Trail, the Anderson Bottom ORV trail spurs left and also continues at the White Rim level to its end. Although both of these trails travel at the White Rim Sandstone level, much of each trail is on relatively recent sediments, or on softer geologic deposits that lie on top of the White Rim.

In many places, however, canyons near the trail cut into the white rock, and the rims of these canyons are bare of sediments, offering endless opportunities for slickrock hiking down into the canyons and along their rims. Upper Big Water Canyon, which the Maze Overlook trail closely parallels for several miles, offers many such places. In one short stretch of this canyon close to the trail, tar seeps out of the rock and builds black cascades and dripping falls on the white sandstone.

On down Big Water Canyon, it cuts more deeply into the older rock, is joined by another drainage and becomes Horse Canyon. A couple of miles beyond this confluence, the ORV trail skirts around the heads of two deep and spectacular tributaries of Horse Canyon, with breathtaking slickrock hiking along their rims and even down into the canyons to intermediate levels.

For further slickrock hiking along the White Rim Sandstone rimlands of the Maze Overlook and Anderson Bottom ORV trails, drive the trails, park wherever the hiking looks good and explore as far as time permits. Such freelance exploring away from the vehicle trails in the Maze area is limited by the amount of water that can be carried, especially during the warmer months, but is highly rewarding because it offers canyon-rim views of this colorful and spectacular country that can be had no other way. Only air-touring can provide a better overview of the intricate canyon systems of The Maze.

Horse Canyon

249

ANOTHER KIND OF SLICKROCK

During the colder months, canyon country displays a kind of slickrock that is absent the rest of the year -- great expanses of ice, frozen water -- where none exist otherwise. This kind of "slickrock" is slick, indeed, and almost as hard as rock.

We were hiking through the winter wonderland of the North Fork of Sevenmile Canyon, amazed at what we were seeing. For most of the year, the bottom of the canyon is largely loose sand and a few slabs of rock, with no signs of water. Bone dry. Yet now the canyon floor was a solid sheet of ice, perhaps twenty feet wide and as much as a foot or more thick!

We pondered this strange phenomenon. Where had that much water come from, in a canyon that saw water only during rare flash-floods? After studying the canyon for several hundred yards, we concluded that it was not as dry as it appeared. The water that flowed its length normally flowed beneath the surface sand, unseen and unsuspected. An upside-down stream.

In the winter, however, when the deeper wet sand froze, the slow water flow was forced to the surface and built up as layer after layer of pure white ice -- a linear frozen pond that continually grew wider and deeper, as long as the winter lasted.

We estimated the length of the natural ice-rink beside which we were hiking. Tiny ice-falls or steps broke the otherwise perfectly smooth, level surface of the ice now and then. Otherwise, it extended upcanyon for about a quarter-mile, unbroken. Then the canyon narrowed and the seep-ice was even more lovely. In the narrows of the upper canyon, where large trees added their sparse winter shade to the already claustrophobic setting, a series of pouroffs created large cascades of winter-sculpted ice.

There we found another oddity, a thick steel cable set into the vertical canyon wall with hot sulfur. This is an old trick for firmly seating metal in rock. An oversized hole is drilled, and the metal rod or cable is inserted into the hole and held there, as molten sulfur is poured in around the metal. Sulfur, unlike most materials, expands on cooling, and thus literally "freezes" the metal very tightly into the rock. But -- getting liquid sulfur into a horizontal hole around a steel cable could not have been easy.

Yet there it was, and the cable stretched upward through the big trees, high above our heads and out of sight toward the opposite canyon rim, a hundred feet or more above. I studied the "hang" of the heavy cable. It could not have been used to lift heavily-laden ore buckets out of the canyon. Too steep. Besides, hauling ore out via the lower canyon would be easier.

What, then? The cable was obviously old. What was going on back then, other than more of the sporadic and largely futile mining that has plagued this unique land since the last century?

We climbed around in the densely vegetated upper canyon, trying to see where the cable went, and perhaps why, and soon my sharp-eyed wife spotted another curious artifact -- two sections of ancient wooden ladder fastened to the cliff, each one offering a way up to a higher ledge, and both leading toward where the mysterious cable disappeared high above.

We couldn't resist. Up we went, but very carefully. The ladders were coated with frost, and the sloping, eroded rock ledges between them were covered with slippery, crusty snow. A fall would not be pleasant. As we reached the top of the second ladder a trail went left round the cliff and along another slippery ledge midway up in a hanging alcove.

The treacherous trail took us to the lower end of a third and much longer ladder, this one badly undercut by erosion. The ladder ended short of the clifftop, but I could see that it was possible to get the rest of the way up by climbing through a large notch in the rimrock. But was the ancient, weathered ladder, with one leg hanging loose at its lower end, secure enough to hold my weight? And would I care to come back down the same way even if it was? What if it gave way? The resulting sliding-drop into the alcove did not look inviting -- and by then we were both chilled to the bone in the deeply shadowed canyon.

That did it! We headed back down. But to "save face" from not having completed this little adventure, for turning chicken in the face of danger, I decided to see if I could find the head of that ladder from the top. It HAD to lead SOMEWHERE!

Back at our vehicle, a half-hour later, we drove out of the canyon to the paved road, then ascended its switchbacks to the higher country between the two forks of Sevenmile. Going by "dead-reckoning," I turned off of the pavement onto a faint ORV trail that seemed to be heading the right direction.

Within a few hundred yards, the trail ended at the brink of North Fork -- and there was the upper end of the cable, stretched across a collapsed frame of heavy timber and anchored in solid rock, again with sulfur.

Finding the upper end of the cable, however, did not answer our questions about its original use, its purpose. That came later, as we asked around among friends who had lived their entire lives in the tiny southeastern Utah community of Moab.

It seems that before the present paved road, Utah 313, had been built, the only way into the higher country to the west was a very long way around -- far to the north, then west, then back south again -- far too long for the stockmen who tended summer herds of livestock in the highlands to go for their occasional supplies. So -- the ranchers had installed a cable that they could use to hoist food and other supplies from a canyon easily reached from Moab, up to hungry men in the higher country -- a canyon country dumbwaiter! Simple -- once you know the answer.

But not so obvious decades later to greenhorns hiking an icy-fantasy canyon in mid-winter. Not obvious at all!

NEEDLES AREA

This geographic area is defined by the Colorado River in the west, Utah 211 and lower Indian Creek in the north, U.S. 191 in the east, and an arbitrary line in the south that includes the northern slopes of the Abajo Mountains.

The perimeter highways and the roads and off-road vehicle trails within the area are described in another *Canyon Country* guidebook and matching map. These are listed by title in each area description and on the inside-back cover of this book.

There are many established hiking trails in the Needles area, most of them within Canyonlands National Park, and some of them crossing considerable slickrock. This book does not cover these established trails, but instead describes some very interesting and challenging freelance slickrock hiking in the Needles area that is not described elsewhere. For more about established trails, hikers are referred to the guidebook, **Canyon Country HIKING and Natural History,** and to National Park Service literature.

NAME - RESORT ROCK

TYPE - route

ROCK - Cutler-Cedar Mesa Sandstone member

USE - hiking only

GUIDEBOOK & MAP - *Canyon Country* OFF-ROAD VEHICLE TRAILS - **Canyon Rims & Needles Areas** and matching map

VEHICLE - highway vehicle

ACCESS

Drive into the Needles District of Canyonlands National Park on Utah 313. Park beside the paved road about 1-1/2 miles inside the park, just before reaching the spur road that goes north to a commercial resort.

254

DESCRIPTION

Hike up onto either of the two arms of red slickrock that end near the road, then continue climbing to higher levels. From there, hike first to the left, toward the long ridge of slickrock that connects this butte with another farther east. Then look for a rock terrace that permits hiking counterclockwise around the still higher sandstone butte. On the south side of the butte, the view down into and beyond the hidden valley there is outstanding, as are the views from anywhere around the butte of other nearby sandstone features of the park.

Along the way around the butte, explore the various levels, alcoves and projecting arms of slickrock. This will serve as an easy but charming introduction to the kind of slickrock hiking that is available everywhere in this general area, one that is accessible to highway vehicles.

NAME - S Q U A W   F L A T

TYPE - area

ROCK - Cutler-Cedar Mesa Sandstone member

USE - hiking only

GUIDEBOOK & MAP - *Canyon Country* OFF-ROAD VEHICLE TRAILS - **Canyon Rims & Needles Areas** and matching map

VEHICLE - highway vehicle

ACCESS

Drive into the Squaw Flat campground in the Needles District of Canyonlands National Park and park anywhere convenient.

DESCRIPTION

The Squaw Flat campground has a number of campsites set in the alcoves and arms of a low mesa of Cedar Mesa Sandstone, making that mesa an excellent place to sample slickrock hiking that is accessible to anyone.

From anywhere feasible in the campground or from its access road, hike up onto the slickrock mesa, then continue exploring its wide top as far west as feasible. This small area is especially lovely at dawn and around sunset, when the low-angle lighting adds even warmer hues to the surrounding meadowlands of Squaw Flat and the nearby fantasyland of sandstone walls and spires.

NAME - DAVIS CANYON

TYPE - areas

ROCK - Cutler-Cedar Mesa Sandstone member

USE - hiking only

GUIDEBOOK & MAP - *Canyon Country* **OFF-ROAD VEHICLE TRAILS - Canyon Rims & Needles Areas** and matching map

VEHICLE - off-road vehicle

ACCESS

Drive south from Moab on U.S. 191, west on Utah 211 toward the Needles District of Canyonlands National Park, then up the Davis Canyon ORV trail, as described in the referenced book and map. Access to the hikable slickrock in this large canyon system begins about 6 miles from the paved road.

Lower Davis Canyon

258

DESCRIPTION

The first and easiest access to the slopes, domes and terraces of Cedar Mesa Sandstone in which this canyon formed begins about a mile before the boundary of Canyonlands National Park is reached, where the gently tilted sandstone layer first rises from the ground. On up the canyon, the sandstone walls become progressively higher. That is because this and other canyons in the areas, such as Titus, Cottonwood, Lavender, Horse, Salt, Lost, Squaw, Big Spring and Elephant, all cut generally into the northern nose of the massive and ancient Monument Uplift, where the upward-arched geologic strata first appear on the surface.

259

Fairly easy access up into the more hikable higher levels of slickrock continues on into the park until the canyon walls become too sheer for easy access except in a few places.

On up the canyon, to and beyond where vehicles are permitted to travel, it becomes continually deeper, making it even more of a challenge to get above the sheer inner-canyon walls to the more gently eroded upper levels, where the slickrock hiking is best. Hikers seeking access to the slickrock highlands this far up the canyon will have to search for ways up by hiking along the walls of the main canyon and up its numerous tributaries.

Once the higher levels of this beautiful sandstone are reached, there is no limit to challenging freelance slickrock hiking. Some of the best such hiking in this delightful canyon system is on the sandstone slopes and ridges in the upper ends of its several tributaries, although getting to these areas requires considerable canyon-bottom hiking.

One special challenge for hikers who enjoy the kind of slickrock hiking this and adjacent canyon systems offer is to look for ways to hike from one canyon floor, up into and across the highlands between canyons, then down into the next canyon. From Davis Canyon, this would be either Lavender or Horse canyons. There is at least one known route between Davis and Lavender canyons, but it is unmarked and cannot be described.

Canyon-to-canyon hiking somewhat complicates vehicular access and egress, and requires some hiking on the younger sediments that cap the ridges some places between the canyons, but is a highly challenging and rewarding adventure, and offers an intimate look at the way this unusually beautiful sandstone erodes. It also provides spectacular views of the canyons and surrounding region that are not found along the area's established hiking routes and trails.

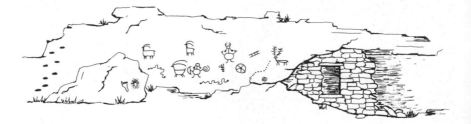

Davis Bridge   Lower Davis Canyon

Prehistoric ruins, Davis Canyon

261

NAME - L A V E N D E R C A N Y O N

TYPE - area

ROCK - Cutler-Cedar Mesa Sandstone member

USE - hiking only

GUIDEBOOK & MAP - *Canyon Country* OFF-ROAD VEHICLE TRAILS - **Canyon Rims & Needles Areas** and matching map

VEHICLE - off-road vehicle

ACCESS

     Drive south from Moab on U.S. 191, west on Utah 211 toward the Needles District of Canyonlands National Park, then up the Lavender Canyon ORV trail, as described in the referenced book and map. Access to the hikable slickrock in this very large canyon system begins about 6 miles from the paved road, in the vicinity of the confluence of the Dry Fork and main branch of Lavender Canyon.

Upper Lavender Canyon -- aerial photo

262

DESCRIPTION

As with many of the other canyons in the Needles District of Canyonlands National Park that cut into the northern upswelling of the Monument Uplift, the sandstone walls of Lavender grow higher and higher as the canyon and its many tributaries are penetrated. One fairly easy place to start slickrock hiking in this canyon system is in the Dry Fork. Its low slickrock walls remain easy to surmount for a considerable distance up the canyon, and there are several interesting natural rock spans there.

The first of these is on the right side very shortly up the canyon. It formed from an opening in the roof of a low cave. The second is a double arch, farther up the canyon and also on the right side, but is hidden behind large shrubs. The third span is on the left side of the canyon and also formed by an opening in a cave roof, but the cave is very wide and deep.

Dry Fork Arch, Lavender Canyon

On up the main branch of Lavender Canyon, there are many more natural spans and a number of prehistoric ruins, but access to the higher levels of slickrock becomes more difficult to find. Even so, one good route up can make accessible an immense area of very hikable slickrock, and can offer the bonus of a possible way across the high ridges between major canyons. There is at least one known route between Lavender and Davis canyons.

On up the main canyon, Caterpillar Arch offers challenging slickrock hiking and climbing. The rock ledges below the arch can be ascended for some distance, and it is possible to reach the top of this large, looping span from the canyon floor via an indirect route that begins downcanyon of the arch.

Another slickrock route that is worth exploring begins in the side-canyon behind immense Cleft Arch, which offers a way up the steeply eroded slickrock to the opening beneath the span. There, the cleft that runs the length of the arch is clearly visible. One of the slickrock ledges in the main canyon below the opening is also interesting to hike. This and several other climbs upward from the canyon floor lead to prehistoric ruins at intermediate slickrock levels.

Cleft Arch -- for scale note tiny figure, bottom-center

As with other nearby canyons, some of the best slickrock hiking is at the upper ends of the canyon's several tributaries, where the upper drainages have carved steeply tilted slickrock mazes, although it takes considerable canyon-bottom hiking to reach these areas. The best way to ascend into and explore these fascinating canyon-heads is to terrace upward to whatever level offers practical lateral exploration.

Altogether, the vertical maze of Cedar Mesa Sandstone from which Lavender Canyon was carved can provide weeks of outstanding slickrock hiking and exploring, along routes and through areas rarely seen by anyone. The best way to do this is from vehicle or backpack base camps at various locations within the canyon.

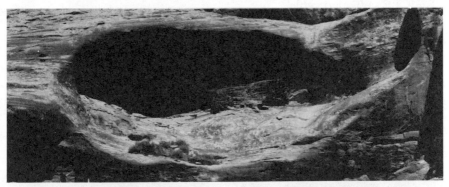

Lavender Canyon cliff-dwelling

Hand Holt Arch   *Caterpillar Arch*

NAME - UPPER SALT CREEK CANYON

TYPE - area

ROCK - Cutler-Cedar Mesa Sandstone member

USE - hiking only

GUIDEBOOK & MAP - *Canyon Country* OFF-ROAD VEHICLE TRAILS - **Canyon Rims & Needles Areas** and matching map

VEHICLE - off-road vehicle

ACCESS

Upper Salt Creek Canyon is defined as that part of the long Salt Creek drainage that is south of the paved road into the park. While the rimlands above the deep gorge of Lower Salt Creek Canyon offer considerable slickrock hiking, this description is limited to the upper canyon. This stretch alone is so long that two practical access routes are described.

Upper Salt Creek Canyon

For access to the lower end of Upper Salt Creek Canyon, drive south from Moab on U.S. 191, west on Utah 211 into the Needles District of Canyonlands National Park, then up the Salt Creek Canyon ORV trail, as described in the referenced book and map. Access to the first hikable slickrock begins about 1/2 mile from the graded dirt road that provides access to the ORV trail.

For access to the upper end of Upper Salt Creek Canyon, drive south from Moab on U.S. 191, west on Utah 211, then up the Cottonwood Canyon ORV trail, as described in the referenced book and map. Continue on this trail to just beyond Cathedral Butte, then turn right onto a short spur trail that ends at the rim above one upper arm of Salt Creek Canyon. Hike down into the canyon via the marked hiking trail that begins there. Exploring via this route is practical only by backpack.

DESCRIPTION

Upper Salt Creek Canyon is vastly more complex that any of the other canyons in the Needles District of the park that cut into the northern end of the Monument Uplift. It thus offers even more opportunities for outstanding slickrock hiking. Because of the canyon's complexity and numerous side-canyons, there are more ways to climb upward into the intermediate and higher levels of slickrock that make the best hiking.

Kirk Arch, Upper Salt Creek Canyon

As in the other nearby canyons that are walled with Cedar Mesa Sandstone, exploring the canyon's slickrock requires considerable canyon-floor hiking or driving between access routes upward. Hikers must also find their own routes up into the best slickrock levels, but the rewards are high. In much of the slickrock highlands above the canyon complex, once the higher, more gently eroded slickrock is reached, entire areas of the beautiful maze of rock are open to exploring. Hikers who confine their explorations of Salt Creek and other similar canyons to the canyon floors are missing the most beautiful, challenging and enchanting aspects of these canyons.

One place where an introduction to this canyon's slickrock hiking is fairly accessible is at popular Angel Arch. The large expanse of rock below the lofty span is worth exploring, and there is an unmarked route up to, through and beyond the span. Views from beneath Angel Arch of the canyon below and the surrounding rock wilderness are outstanding.

Beyond Angel Arch -- for scale note figure beneath span

As with Davis and Lavender canyons, there are numerous pre-historic dwellings and granaries in rock alcoves and on ledges above the Salt Creek Canyon floor. Although such protected archaeological remnants should not be entered or disturbed in any way, their presence generally indicates that there is a nearby route up from the canyon floor, and some such routes can be used to gain higher, more hikable slickrock levels.

For an introduction to the potential slickrock hiking in the upper end of Upper Salt Creek Canyon, drive or hike to the end of the Big Pocket Overlook ORV trail that spurs out between upper arms of Salt Creek and Lavender canyons from the base of Cathedral Butte, about 3/4 mile before the head of the hiking trail into Salt Creek Canyon. Adventurous backpackers might enjoy the challenge of descending into the canyon from this elevated viewpoint. There is a proven route down that reaches the canyon floor and the main hiking trail in the vicinity of Kirks Cabin, an historic structure that is visible from above with binoculars.

From Big Pocket Overlook, the panorama below of the upper reaches of Salt Creek and adjacent canyons is breathtaking. There is nothing like it elsewhere in the park vicinity. The tremendous expanse of weathered, colorful red-and-white-banded Cedar Mesa slickrock is almost unbelievable. Careful study of this intricate maze from various stretches of the viewpoint's elevated rim will reveal several large arches, some near the canyon floor, others in higher slickrock levels. Reaching some of the higher spans can be quite challenging.

As in the lower end of Upper Salt Creek Canyon, there are endless opportunities for attaining the intermediate and higher slickrock slopes and terraces, and innumerable spur canyons to explore, many of them eroded from solid rock. Also, as in the lower canyon, considerable canyon-floor hiking is necessary between access points up into the slickrock, but once this is reached, extensive areas of outstanding slickrock hiking become available.

Again, the only practical way to explore the vastness of this slickrock area is from base camps, and literally months can be spent in this area alone without exhausting its slickrock hiking potential.

NAME - HORSE CANYON

TYPE - area

ROCK - Cutler-Cedar Mesa Sandstone member

USE - hiking only

GUIDEBOOK & MAP - *Canyon Country* OFF-ROAD VEHICLE TRAILS - **Canyon Rims & Needles Areas** and matching map

VEHICLE - off-road vehicle

ACCESS

For access to the lower end of Horse Canyon, drive south from Moab on U.S. 191, west on Utah 211 into the Needles District of Canyonlands National Park, up the Salt Creek Canyon ORV trail, then up the Horse Canyon ORV trail, as described in the referenced book and map. Access to the first hikable slickrock begins immediately.

Gothic Arch

DESCRIPTION

Within about 1-1/2 miles of where Horse Canyon branches from Salt Creek Canyon, a spur ORV trail into a side-canyon offers a first sampling of slickrock hiking. There, to get near Tower Ruin, it is necessary to climb the steep slopes of rock below the prehistoric structure. Nearby Paul Bunyans Potty, a gigantic pothole arch high in the side-canyon's left cliffline, also presents a challenge to slickrock hikers. It is possible, but not easy, to get into the immense alcove behind the span, where there are remnants of prehistoric structures.

On up the main canyon, there are numerous routes up into the sloping, terraced slickrock that offers the best hiking. Getting to lofty Gothic Arch can be a challenge, but reaching good viewpoints of graceful Castle Arch and massive Fortress Arch is easier. Getting to the arches themselves is another matter.

Paul Bunyans Potty   Castle Arch

Horse Canyon is much smaller than either Lavender or Salt canyons, but still provides ample opportunities for challenging slickrock hiking through enchanting areas and to unique goals. As with all the nearby canyons, hiking their bottoms only, while well worth doing, is barely an introduction to the total beauty and novelty the canyons offer. Slickrock hiking provides access to the full potential of these geologically incomparable canyons.

Because of its more limited size, it is practical to explore much of Horse Canyon from a base camp in the Squaw Flat campground, if an off-road vehicle is available for driving up the canyon each day, but backpack camps save travel time and offer the bonus of a superior wilderness experience.

Fortress Arch

Horse Canyon Narrows

273

THE PURPLE PLAYA RIFT

We were hiking along the rimlands of the North Fork of Mill Creek, awestruck by its varied beauty and, as always, looking for anomalies in the Navajo Sandstone that makes up its sheer walls and wildly eroded rims. We were especially alert, because only recently we had discovered an area that contained countless curious tracks made by some kind of tiny prehistoric creature in one of the numerous "petrified playas" so common in this rock.

As we approached a deep crevice in the rim, we noticed that beside the rim was a ridge of odd-colored, layered rock that was somewhat harder and weathered into peculiar shapes. We soon saw, as we explored along this odd outcrop, that this was another ancient desert playa, a place in an otherwise barren, arid desert where rare rain-water had collected before quickly evaporating.

Only this playa was somewhat different. Because its general color was somewhat purple-hued, we quickly dubbed it "The Purple Playa." We both love alliterative names. After exploring the remains of this oddity for several hundred feet, until it ended between two other deep but more open clefts, we returned to the first cleft and started scrambling down into its dark depths.

The first few yards were rubble and sandy sediments, barely held in place by sparse vegetation and larger rocks and a bit of exposed slickrock. Then the going got rougher, and even steeper, as the sheer walls, just a few feet apart, rose higher above us.

Shortly, we spotted an arch of sorts clinging high on one wall. It seemed like we might be able to get quite near it from above. We planned to try that later, but for now were intent on seeing how far we could get down the rapidly narrowing cleft. Would we be able to get all the way down into North Fork? If so, it would be the second such hidden route into the 400-foot gorge from its forbidding rim that we had discovered in recent times. The other route was in the vicinity of Otho Natural Bridge.

We were not to succeed in getting all the way down. About halfway or more down, we guessed, the cleft narrowed to a slot barely four feet wide, and that was blocked by a large boulder! There was too little room to crawl beneath the boulder, and it was too far to jump down beyond the boulder -- and then expect to get back up if we had to retreat up the cleft.

So we gave up, for then. But not forever. We returned for a better organized try a few weeks later, this time with two friends, somewhat younger and more agile than ourselves, and with a length of climbing rope. Since we expected to get all the way down to the North Fork, and then hike the long way around to our vehicle, two of us carried day-packs containing lunches. I carried the rope and a camera.

We made easy progress to the blocking boulder, then attached our rope to a handy tree above it for the short rappel beyond the blockage. After all four had descended, we pulled the rope after us. The more nimble one of our crew planned to free-climb back up and attach the rope again if we had to turn back.

The cleft next narrowed so that in places it was necessary for those carrying day-packs to take them off and slip sideways in order to make further progress, and we made another short drop or two that had handy crevices for climbing down -- or back up. Then we came to an undercut drop, this one with no convenient toe-holds, and with no place to attach our rope.

Experienced rock climbers would have had no trouble continuing, but while we all could at least do a short rappel down, none of us had the strength or skill necessary to chimney down the narrow slot that we faced, or to ascend back up a rope held by someone, with no toe-holds to help.

We were aid-hikers, not climbers, and the smooth-walled slot and ten-foot drop that we faced was simply too much for us, even though it seemed as though we were almost all the way down to where the remaining descent to the creek would be just scrambling down a series of typical Kayenta ledges. We were all keenly disappointed -- but the story does have a happy ending.

Several years later, during a period of extreme drought, I was asked by the leader of a group of young survival-type back-packers where they might find a wild canyon that still had some water, and that offered a variety of hiking challenges. I aimed them at North Fork, and during my map-talk told them about my slot-canyon route between the perennial creek and the erosional wonders in its lofty rimlands. I told them that climbing rope and chimneying skills would be necessary for the trip up or down.

A week later, the leader reported that his group had conquered our frustrating slot-canyon. They were possibly the first ever to do so. My wife and I enjoyed a bit of vicarious satisfaction. Maybe someday, even yet --

SLICKROCK AREAS
ELSEWHERE IN SOUTHERN UTAH

The slickrock areas and routes listed and described in this book are far from being the only hikable, bikable slickrock within the canyon country region defined by the Abajo Mountains, Utah 24, Interstate 70 and the Utah-Colorado border. There are also many other excellent locations within the general Four Corners region, especially within southern Utah and its borderlands with Arizona and Colorado.

For hikers and bikers who have learned to enjoy the unique recreational potential of sandstone slickrock, following is a list of other general slickrock areas. It should be noted that most of the areas listed are far from settlements of any size. Thus, careful planning is essential to their exploration. Those planning to explore slickrock areas within Indian reservations are required by tribal policy to obtain permits in advance. These are available at various tribal offices. Reservation boundaries are shown on most state and regional maps.

AREAS AND TYPES OF SANDSTONE

The Colorado River - San Juan River Triangle - Navajo Sandstone

The area between Boulder and Escalante, Utah - Navajo Sandstone

The Grand Gulch, Slickhorn, Owl/Fish Creek rimlands - Cedar Mesa

Comb Ridge - Navajo Sandstone

The San Rafael Reef - several formations

The Monument Valley vicinity - deChelly Sandstone

The Capitol Reef-Waterpocket Fold area - several formations

Lake Powell, Padre Bay peninsulas - Entrada Slickrock equivalent

AUTHOR'S FAVORITE AREAS AND ROUTES

Choosing a few favorite slickrock areas from the hundreds my wife and I have hiked over the last two decades is like choosing a few favorite foods when you enjoy them all, each for its own unique texture, aroma and flavor. Our subjective enjoyment of each slickrock area also changes with the season, with the local weather, the time of day, the amount of precipitation that has fallen recently, our personal moods and the reasons why we are hiking -- whether primarily for pleasure, or for taking pictures for this and other publications, or to introduce friends to the unique nature of exploring the intricate beauty of slickrock.

Thus, the following list of slickrock areas should not be taken as the only ones worth exploring, but as those which I would least like to lose to industrial development, areas that my wife and I have returned to time and time again, that well illustrate the extraordinary nature of slickrock hiking and biking.

Here, then, are a few places where novices to these two recreational pursuits might begin. Some of the listed areas are good for both hiking and biking. See individual descriptions for details.

Eye-of-the-Whale Mesa

FAVORITE HIKING AREAS AND ROUTES
in alphabetical sequence

OUTSTANDING BIKING AREAS AND ROUTES
in alphabetical sequence

A NEW SPORT

It isn't every day that you discover a new sport. No, I don't mean some novel kind of competitive athletic endeavor. I mean "sport" as in biological mutation, in this case botanical.

We recently spotted a bright lemon-yellow branch on one otherwise normal specimen of the exotic shrub, tamarisk, not far beyond the Hunter Canyon drainage in Cane Creek Canyon, but we found our first native sport several years ago, while first hiking the south rim of Bartlett Wash.

My wife and I were quite far along this high, sloping wall of reddish Entrada slickrock, somewhat beyond the first place where it becomes necessary to climb to the lofty terrace that marks the interface between the Moab and Slickrock members of the Entrada. We were still on the broad, tree-studded bench there, headed toward the skyscraping narrow ridge that separates Bartlett and upper Tusher, when one of us spotted a peculiarity, a twisted juniper tree that somehow didn't look quite right.

On close examination, it surely wasn't normal. Its general shape was what we had come to expect in this ancient, hardy species, but its usual sparse, spatulate spreads of foliage were definitely abnormal. Rather than its green clusters being sparse and open, they were tightly bunched, in dense clumps, over the entire tree, like something very familiar -- but what?

After a few moments examining this strange specimen of juniper, we decided to give it a name that would describe the tree's unique foliage. We called our sport *Junipero broccoli.* Don't look for it in tree-books.

Some day I'm going to go back and photograph that odd tree for the record -- if I can find it. Maybe you can.

INDEX OF PERSONAL ANECDOTES

INDEX OF BIKABLE AREAS AND ROUTES

Eric Bajon photo

INDEX OF AREAS
ACCESSIBLE TO HIGHWAY VEHICLES

NAME	PAGE

Sand Flats area

ACKNOWLEDGMENTS

This book is a compilation of some of the slickrock hiking experiences of a very compatible husband-and-wife team over a period of two decades. In that sense, Terby, my wife and lifetime partner in all the adventures, good and bad, that we have endured and enjoyed over our married life, is co-author of this book.

She has walked and hiked on, climbed up and down, scrambled through, around and over, or slid down every inch of slickrock that I have. She has helped give human perspective to many of this book's photographs. She has also discussed the subject of the book with me at its conceptual stage, reviewed my first outline of its contents, edited its various drafts, and proof-read its final printout before typesetting, all with outstanding skill and infinite patience.

To her, my heartfelt *"Thanks! I could not have done this book without you!"* Nor would I have had the incentive -- to walk the rock or write the book.

At various stages of the book's creation, others have also offered their invaluable help. Our dear friend and computer-whiz, Tom Budlong of Los Angeles, helped us finally conquer lofty Skywalk Arch and coined the term "skywalking," as cheerfully and efficiently as he earlier helped us check out parts of the historic Macomb expedition route through remote wilderness lands.

Our young friend, Marilyn Peterson, who is a happy hiker, a rock climber and mountain-biking enthusiast, helped us check out one slickrock biking area and provided a photogenic element to several pictures of both slickrock hiking and biking, as did several others who have come to appreciate the novel joys and challenges of slickrock biking.

My sincere thanks, also, to Julie Howard, for sharing with us her secret route up onto Mill-Tusher Mesa, and to the sturdy pinyon tree near the top that made that route practical.

To all these, and others too numerous to list, my hearty --

"Thanks! By your efforts, you helped create this book."

Fran Barnes

ALPHABETICAL INDEX
OF LISTED AREAS AND ROUTES

NAME   PAGE

WHAT'S A GIRL TO DO?

For many years we seldom went hiking without our little mongrel dog -- half Scottie, half Dachshund, would you believe? Her name was Token -- she was black and the only dog among our extended family of cats -- and thus a "token" cat. She was short and wiry and homely, but loved to hike with us -- except on slickrock. The rough surface of sandstone was tough on her feet.

Still, she insisted on going along wherever we went, and usually did fine, although during hot weather her chosen route was the shortest distance between patches of shade, and on longer hikes she often had to be carried back to the vehicle.

But once, a slickrock hike posed a special problem for our little black girl-dog.

We were slowly ascending the wide, sloping surface of a huge sandstone fin in the Klondike Ridge area. The day was warm and bright but not hot, so Token was doing fine, running ahead as she usually did and this time, since there was only one route up the fin, not misreading where we were going and continually dashing off in the wrong direction.

She was a few yards ahead of us up the fairly steep slope of smooth sandstone, when suddenly she paused and began to search anxiously around. We stopped and watched her, to see what had interested a dog on this barren slickrock. Certainly not one of the rabbits that she loved to chase but never caught. What desert rabbit in its right mind would frequent bare rock?

After a few seconds of frantic circling, Token paused and assumed a familiar posture for a few seconds, then looked back down at us embarrassedly -- while we broke up watching a small brown ovoid roll rapidly past us and on down the slickrock fin.

What else is a girl to do when she simply has to go -- on a smooth sandstone slope?

BIBLIOGRAPHY

Ballard, Robert D., **Exploring Our Living Planet,** National Geographic
     Society, 1988
Barnes, F. A., *Canyon Country* **GEOLOGY,** Wasatch Publishers, 1978
------ *Canyon Country* **HIGHWAY TOURING,** Four Corners Publications,
     1988
------ *Canyon Country* **ARCHES & BRIDGES,** Canyon Country Publica
     tions, 1987
------ *Canyon Country* **OFF-ROAD VEHICLE TRAILS - Arches & La Sals
     Areas,** Canyon Country Publications, 1989
------ *Canyon Country* **OFF-ROAD VEHICLE TRAILS - Canyon Rims &
     Needles Areas,** Canyon Country Publications, 1987
------ *Canyon Country* **OFF-ROAD VEHICLE TRAILS - Island Area,**
     Canyon Country Publications, 1988
------ *Canyon Country* **OFF-ROAD VEHICLE TRAIL MAP - Arches & La
     Sals Areas,** Wasatch Publishers, 1986
------ *Canyon Country* **OFF-ROAD VEHICLE TRAIL MAP - Canyon
     Rims & Needles Areas,** Wasatch Publishers, 1986
------ *Canyon Country* **OFF-ROAD VEHICLE TRAIL MAP - Island Area,**
     Wasatch Publishers, 1989
------ *Canyon Country* **OFF-ROAD VEHICLE TRAIL MAP - Maze Area,**
     Canyon Country Publications, 1988
Barnes & Kuehne, *Canyon Country* **MOUNTAIN BIKING,** Canyon
     Country Publications, 1988
Bickers, Jack, *Canyon Country* **OFF-ROAD VEHICLE TRAILS - Maze
     Area,** Canyon Country Publications, 1988
------ **THE LABYRINTH RIMS - 60 Accesses to Green River Overlooks,**
     4-WD Trailguides Publications, 1988
Doelling, Hellmut H., **Geologic Map of Arches National Park and
     Vicinity,** Utah Geological and Mineral Survey, 1985
Hintze, Lehi F., **Geologic History of Utah,** Department of Geology,
     Brigham Young University, 1988
Huntoon, Peter W., et al, **Geologic Map of Canyonlands National Park
     and Vicinity,** Canyonlands Natural History Association, 1982
Redfern, Ron, **The Making of a Continent,** Times Books, 1983
Stokes, W. Lee, **Geology of Utah,** Utah Museum of Natural History and
     Utah Geological and Mineral Survey, 1986

FURTHER READING

Hikers and bikers who wish to know more about the unique and fascinating canyon country of southeastern Utah will find other books and maps in the *Canyon Country* series both useful and informative. They are stocked by many visitor centers and retail outlets in the region.

The listed books are profusely illustrated with photographs, charts, graphs, maps and original artwork. The maps are also illustrated with representative photographs.

GENERAL INFORMATION

Canyon Country HIGHWAY TOURING by F. A. Barnes. A guide to the highways and roads in the region that can safely be traveled by highway vehicles, plus descriptions of all the national and state parks and monuments and other special areas in the region.

Canyon Country EXPLORING by F. A. Barnes. A brief history of early explorations, plus details concerning the administration of this vast area of public land and exploring the region today by land, air and water.

Canyon Country CAMPING by F. A. Barnes. A complete guide to all kinds of camping in the region, including highway pull-offs, developed public and commercial campgrounds, and backcountry camping from vehicles and backpacks.

Canyon Country GEOLOGY by F. A. Barnes. A summary of the unique geologic history of the region for the general reader, with a list of its unusual land-forms and a section on rock collecting.

Canyon Country PREHISTORIC INDIANS by Barnes & Pendleton. A detailed description of the region's two major prehistoric Indian cultures, with sections telling where to view their ruins, rock art and artifacts.

Canyon Country PREHISTORIC ROCK ART by F. A. Barnes. A comprehensive study of the mysterious prehistoric rock art found throughout the region, with a section listing places where it can be viewed.

Canyon Country ARCHES & BRIDGES by F. A. Barnes. A complete description of the unique natural arches, bridges and windows found throughout the region, with hundreds depicted.

UTAH CANYON COUNTRY by F. A. Barnes. An overview of the entire region's natural and human history, parks and monuments, and recreational opportunities, illustrated in full color.

CANYONLANDS NATIONAL PARK - *Early History & First Descriptions* by F. A. Barnes. A summary of the early history of this uniquely spectacular national park, including quotes from the journals of the first explorers to see and describe it.

Canyon Country's CANYON RIMS RECREATION AREA by F. A. and M. M. Barnes. A description of the natural and human history and outstanding scenic beauty in this immense area to the east of Canyonlands National Park, plus a summary of its outstanding recreational opportunities.